"The bewildering pace in which w[illegible]
rate of human development. Thos[illegible] an age of reconciliation' where we will create a balance between ourselves and other aspects of our lives, be it job, marriage, finances, or spirituality. *Walking the Tightrope* provides a stepwise guide to this change. The authors gently, through their own self-disclosure, support the reader in a realistic commitment to a balance of the 'self.'"

—Dr. Phil Heller, Clinical and Forensic Psychologist

"In their new book, *Walking the Tightrope*, Erica Orloff and Kathy Levinson are daring high wire artists who offer hope on a rope by helping us put the balance back into our three-ring circus lives. They show us how to map success and to chart life courses that are fulfilling and dynamic. By helping us clear up our fuzzy thinking, they focus us on creating solutions that become foundational blueprints for our new lives. If you are at the end of your rope, don't despair because Orloff and Levinson throw us a lifeline with their down-to-earth, commonsense approach to finding exciting equilibriums for our hearts and souls and for making change last for us and the ones we love."

—Ronald J. Chenail, Ph.D., Assistant to the President for Academic Affairs, Nova Southeastern University

"This book is about simplifying life's complexities to find balance in our harried, fast-paced world. Orloff and Levinson guide us in how to actively take control of what we can control with concrete strategies, mindfulness, and respect for ourselves."

—Edmund C. Neuhaus, Ph.D., Harvard Medical School and McLean Hospital

"What a large, therapeutic journey to capture life and its core . . . Not only are [the authors] clear and organized in [their] plan for balance, while simultaneously teasing through the fluff, but [their] personal vignettes of the numerous 'insane Kodak moments' we all share has given me room to breath, anew. I am comforted knowing my journey for balance is a shared world view."

—Marcy Sirkin, Ph.D., Family Therapist

Walking the Tightrope

Walking the Tightrope

Erica Orloff

Kathy Levinson

PEARSON
Prentice Hall

PRENTICE HALL
An Imprint of Pearson Education
Upper Saddle River, NJ New York London San Francisco Toronto
Sydney Tokyo Singapore Hong Kong Cape Town Madrid Paris
Milan Munich Amsterdam
www.ft-ph.com

A CIP catalogue record for this book can be obtained from the Library of Congress.

Orloff, Erica.
Walking the tightrope : coping with the demands of our modern life/Erica Orloff, Kathy Levinson.
p. cm.
ISBN 0-13-142024-0
1. Conduct of life. I Levinson, Kathy. II. Title.

BJ1581.2.067 2004
158--dc22

2003027869

Editorial/production supervision: *Patty Donovan*
Composition: *Pine Tree Composition*
Cover Design Director: *Jerry Votta*
Art Director: *Gail Cocker-Bogusz*
Manufacturing Manager: *Alexis Heydt-Long*
Manufacturing Buyer: *Maura Zaldivar*
VP, Executive Editor: *Tim Moore*
Editorial Assistant: *Richard Winkler*
Development Editor: *Russ Hall*
Marketing Manager: John Pierce
Full Servioe Production Manager: *Anne R. Garcia*

Publishing as Prentice Hall
Upper Saddle River, New Jersey 07458

The publisher offers excellent discounts on this book when ordered in quantity for bulk purchases or special sales.
For more information, please contact:

U.S. Corporate and Government Sales
1-800-382-3419
corpsales@pearsontechgroup.com

For sales outside of the U.S., please contact:

International Sales
1-317-581-3793
international@pearsontechgroup.com

Printed in the United States of America
First Printing

ISBN 0-13-142024-0

Pearson Education LTD.
Pearson Education Australia PTY, Limited
Pearson Education Singapore, Pte. Ltd.
Pearson Education North Asia Ltd.
Pearson Education Canada, Ltd.
Pearson Educación de Mexico, S.A. de C.V.
Pearson Education—Japan
Pearson Education Malaysia, Pte. Ltd.
Pearson Education, Upper Saddle River, New Jersey

EO—For my mother, Maryanne Orloff, who somehow balanced three kids and work and even managed to cook gourmet meals while she was at it. I obviously did not inherit the cooking gene.

*KL—For Master Kwon,
a living example that through dedication, discipline, and passion comes excellence.*

CONTENTS

PREFACE

We all grew up with a dream that technology was going to make our lives better. The computer was going to make our jobs faster and easier. The fax would let us zip a memo across the globe in the time it took to dial a phone number. Email was going to let us keep in touch with friends and family members when we had no time to compose an old-fashioned letter or even to make a 10-minute long-distance phone call. We could give up playing phone tag and press the Send button instead.

What happened?

Instead of making our lives simpler, we are living in the first generation of the 24/7 millennium and all that concept entails. We're wired to the point of exhaustion; we're fractured and frazzled. We wear our cell phones on our hips and complain when legislation demands we get a hands-free headset for our car—when ten years ago we barely even dreamed of talking from the freeway. Our kids have cell phones, our boss expects us to answer email at 11:00 at night, and most of us take our laptops on vacation so we can wire in to the office in case there's an emergency. We're being instant messaged to death. And we're suffering from burnout. A lot of us wonder about that old Peggy Lee standard, "Is that all there is?"

Then September 11 happened. The unthinkable descended on our nation, terrorism hit our shores, and over 2,000 people left for the office or hopped on a plane never to return. Suddenly, we all examined words like "family time" and "balance" in a new light. For those of us who have had to board a plane post–September 11 for our jobs, the idea of leaving home became frightening. We were panicked and tired. Many of us talked about slowing down, taking time to tuck our kids in, soothe a child frightened by nightmares, pursue our dreams, find a deeper purpose in our lives, find something greater than ourselves to resonate with. We swore we would change . . . And most of us haven't.

As the economy slid into a recession, as the reality of having to make a living collided with the idea of more free time, we were just as wired as before. So are we a nation pushing closer and closer to burnout across the board? And what can we do about it?

This book is about balance. It's about bringing yourself back from the brink of burnout and helping you connect to those things that are most important to you—whether that be hearth and home or an avocation or passion to follow a dream. We're going to bring six areas of your life into clear focus and help you figure out what you need to balance the following:

1. Your financial life

2. Your work life

3. Your relationships—with significant other, family, friends and professional peers

4. Your health

5. Your social world

6. Your spiritual life

Each chapter will offer a quiz and questions to help you see if you are "out of balance" in that area, as well as some incisive questions that will bring into focus what you *really* want for that area. Next we'll tackle some concrete, practical, real-life advice about how to attain balance. We also include a chapter on diagnosing when you're slipping back into bad habits and old routines that will lead you back into the 24/7 rut.

Most important, this book is about real life—yours and ours. We see the other self-help gurus out there. Sure, it would be nice to go off to expensive spas and ashrams and contemplate life, to be able to unhook and unplug. But the reality is that we need to UNWIRE our own inner selves. We have to be able to find balance within the realm of technology, to carve out a little space that is our own, without saying the heck with cell phones, email, and laptops. We have to be able to earn a living and in light of the fact that the dot.com explosion has gone kaput, it's less likely any of us will become instant millionaires—playing Lotto aside. We're back to building careers and success the old-fashioned way—with hard work, long hours, and ingenuity.

We can't pitch our cell phone into the toilet. We can't abandon our email. We *can* find some balance so that the "wired" parts of our life aren't overtaking the "unwired" parts, so that we actually find five minutes to take care of ourselves.

You need this book if:

- ▲ You can't remember your last vacation, or the only vacation you've taken in the last year involved checking in with the office every morning and afternoon.
- ▲ You don't routinely take time out for yourself. Time out does not include "answering your email," returning phone calls, or anything connected to the office. Time out is pure unadulterated time for yourself.
- ▲ You watch six months go by and realize you haven't spent enough one-on-one time with the important people in your life.
- ▲ You show signs of serious career or emotional burnout, such as intense fatigue, poorly controlled bursts of anger or weepiness, insomnia, lack of focus, unexplained depression, feeling so stressed that you routinely have panic attacks or heart palpitations, and so on.
- ▲ You no longer "dream" about anything more future-oriented than what to make for dinner or when your next presentation is.
- ▲ Your travel or job demands are crowding out the hobbies, people, and ideas most important to you.

Maybe you never had a life in balance . . . maybe you did once but now you're so wired that it's out of control. The time is now to take it back. If there's one thing September 11 showed this nation, it's the fragility of existence. People who have serious illnesses or have come back from devastating crises often report how their lives flashed before their lives. Sometimes they're never the same and they treat each day as a gift. But eventually, for many, that close-to-death experience fades in consciousness and it's back at work, back at the daily grind. Back to a life out of balance.

One final note . . . this isn't a passive book. It requires you to dig deep and answer many questions honestly. But by the end, you should be moving toward personal fulfillment and a life a little less wired.

Erica Orloff

Kathy Levinson

Acknowledgments

We would like to thank our agent, Jay Poynor, of the Poynor Group. Meeting you in Los Angeles was one of the best things that could ever happen. Your loyalty and dedication are unwavering. In the greatest city in the world, you are it.

Once again, we would like to thank Tim Moore, Vice President of Prentice Hall/Financial Times. A seasoned pro in the world of publishing, his insights were always right on.

We thank our editor, Russ Hall, for guiding us to a finished manuscript and for arranging the technical reviews. You may be the hardest-working guy at Prentice Hall.

On a personal note, Erica would like to thank her circle of friends—my co-author and pal Kathy, my "other Kathy" Johnson, Cleo, Nancy, Pammie, Chris Richardson (dahl)—her family, and especially her children, Alexa, Nicholas, and Isabella. Because if I didn't have a reason for finding balance, I would be a workaholic and none of it would have meaning. I'm still a workaholic . . . but I'm learning to balance on the tightrope every day because of you three. And as long as you're reading this, clean your rooms.

On a personal note, Kathy would like to thank her corner of the world—Marc, Peter, and Aimee. Marc, for your unflagging support and patience. You are always there. To my two knuckleheads, Peter and Aimee, who stay up too late and squabble too much, for staying away from the computer. For our giant Mastiff, Ming, for only resting his sopping wet drooling face on my manuscript once.

Kathy would also like to thank NYPD SCUBA's own Tommy Beirne for his support and encouragement. You are a dedicated writer whose time is coming.

CHAPTER 1

DO YOU NEED BALANCE? A BLUEPRINT FOR A STRONG FOUNDATION

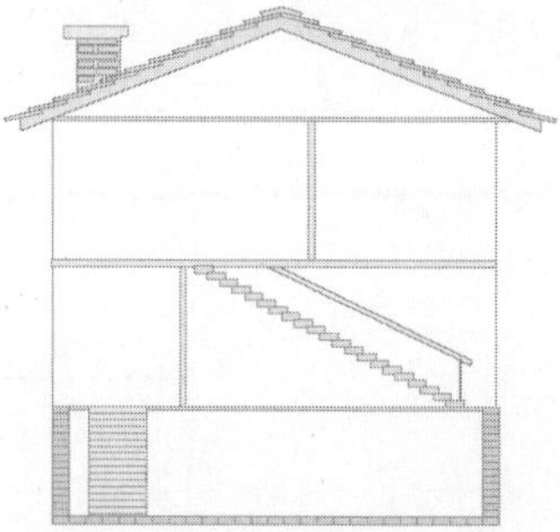

There's that old adage that no one ever said on his or her deathbed, "Gee, I wish I'd put more time in at the office." However, for most of us building a professional life, the office has a tendency to take over our lives, leaving us out of focus and out of balance.

Two other aspects come into this out-of-balance scenario. One is when our worklives are not our passions. Many of us start down a career path and find ourselves 10 or 20 years later with an enviable position and title on a business card—but somehow along the way we may have gotten into a track where we're not truly happy and most certainly not passionate about what we do. Consequently, when most of us spend more hours on the job than at home, we feel frazzled and burned out—we spend too many hours pursuing something that leaves us less than satisfied.

The other side of this coin is that our work may be such a consuming passion for us that we find ourselves in burned-out marriages or poor health because we neglect all the other areas of our life. We may pursue our careers with a single-mindedness that excludes some of the other satisfying aspects of life. We even have a name for this phenomenon—they call us "Road Warriors."

Add to both of these situations a sluggish economy and you have people feeling they have to put in long hours and run up those frequent flyer miles on business trips because in this climate, there aren't as many great jobs from which to choose. Fear is a powerful motivator.

Life As a House

Imagine your life as a house with rooms for all the different areas of your life.

Draw a house of your own. Each room represents something important to you. These rooms should include:

▲ *Job:* Are you working more hours than you want or should be? Is your job your dream job or have you found yourself in a position and on a track that isn't providing you with the career passion you want? Have you stagnated at work? Do you like the people you work with? Is your commute out of control—two hours one way on the train isn't unheard of in large metropolitan areas like New York and Washington, DC. Is your job a source of unending stress that follows you home at night? Is your boss or supervisor reasonable or a bully? Is your company in danger of going under? Has the staff at work been cut down with no replacements hired, thus forcing you to do the work of two people—or more? Are you fairly compensated? You will make this room reasonably sized if things feel "about right" in your career, but if it's out of alignment, then this will take up much more room than you like. It might feel like a monster-sized family room that at its heart is cold, without enough furniture to fill it.

- *Finances:* Are you drowning in debt? Are you saving for the future? Do you have a reasonable retirement plan? Do you have a life insurance policy (even stay-at-home Moms and Dads need to make provisions should something happen to them)? This room will be reasonable if your finances feel in control. It will be large if it's a source of high stress.
- *Children/Created Families:* Have your kids hit the teen years, and are hormones ruling your house? Are you struggling to find time for your kids? Do you have stepchildren and a blended family with some of the bumps in the road it can bring? Do any of your children face any of the following—attention deficit disorder, developmental delays, or illness? Are your kids just as burned out by the pace of the 21st century as you are? Some of us may not have kids, but we may have some form of an extended family, aging parents, and other family issues to confront. Draw this room accordingly.
- *Marriage/Significant Other:* Do you devote the time and attention needed to keep the passion and joy in your relationship alive? Is your spouse or significant other neglected because of the demands of your career and vice versa?
- *Friends/Social Life:* Do you have time to keep up with the friends in your life? Do you even have the kind of special friends you can call with a crisis at 2:00 in the morning? Do you get to enjoy a social life or does work eat up most of your free time? Include here hobbies that you enjoy.
- *Spiritual Life:* Whether this is church, synagogue, mosque, or going outside and hugging a tree, your life and "house" should include time for spiritual pursuits such as prayer, meditation, or reflection.
- *Issues/Baggage (what from the past still brings you down?):* This room *should* be small, if the issues from the past have been dealt with and

no longer bring you down. This will grow in size if issues such as alcoholism in your family of origin, abuse as a child, or simply an unhappy home life as a kid continue to follow you into adulthood and cause you pain.

- *Community/Volunteering:* If you haven't considered the joys of volunteering because you have no time, this may be something to look at. For many, volunteering is a source of great personal satisfaction. This may be something you've always wanted to do, but that little problem of there only being 24 hours in a day keeps getting in the way. This room will be a sliver if you don't volunteer and wish you could.
- *Health and Well-Being:* Do you exercise a minimum of four times a week? We all know what we *should* do in terms of eating right, cutting back on caffeine, avoiding too much alcohol, not smoking, and so forth, but sometimes the stress of life causes us to not take care of ourselves. Again, this room will feel "right" if it's an appropriate portion of the house. If it's really tiny, that's a sign of trouble.

And finally, the room that's often just the size of a closet:

- *Self:* Yes. Time for YOU. (What's that, you may be asking. If that's the case, draw this super small.)

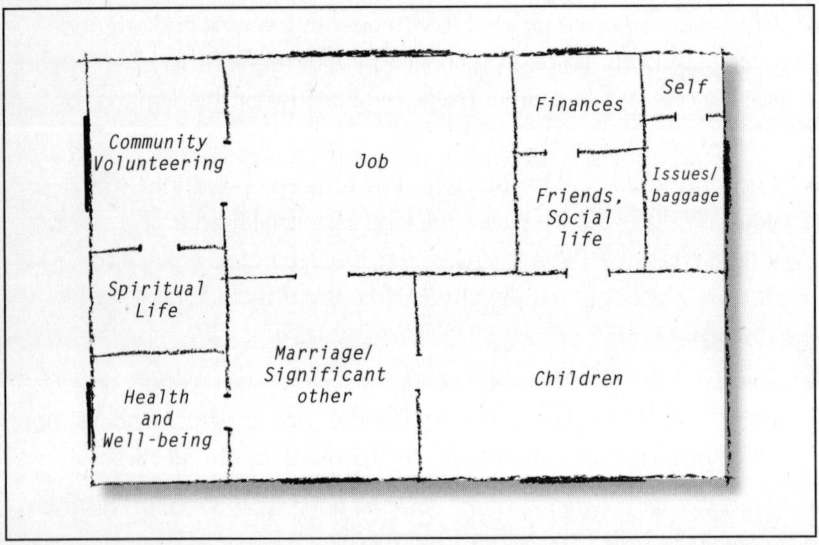

Take a look at your house. If you've been honest and carefully considered the proportions, you may be shocked to find that your job consumes the biggest share. Though you may want your family or significant other to have "big rooms," the way you're constantly moving from work to the drive-thru for dinner to the soccer field for your daughter's game, rushing home to check email, then hurriedly getting the kids to bed so you can plan for tomorrow may cause their rooms to be smaller than you'd like. Worst of all, "self" may be so tiny as to be negligible. When was the last time you did something just for you, like took a course because it interested you, invested in a hobby, or just read for pleasure, instead of using your time to prepare for a key meeting at work?

If self is so small for most of us, it's not a wonder that we often ask, "Is that all there is?" in life. Abraham Maslow, one of the greatest minds in 20th-century psychology, said we all innately strive to become "self-actualized." A self-actualized human being has met all his or her preliminary "needs" along the way in life. This person has shelter, food, and clothing; has found true love; has met his or her social needs in the community; has found satisfaction in life itself; and now feels complete, or actualized. However, the only way to achieve this state is to have time for self and to be able to examine inwardly. Without time for self, we neglect the person who should be the most important in our own life—ourself.

Wherever You Go, There You Are

Look around you. Wherever you go, there you are (which also happens to be the theme line from the 1984 classic *Buckaroo Bonzai*). What does that mean? Try as you might, you can't avoid taking yourself with you. In other words, you run through life at breakneck speed, too busy to really *look* at whether or not you are satisfied with life, and the speed factor helps you to continue to avoid looking. Then something happens. For some people it was September 11, which forced them to really examine whether all the attention on career and even material values was worth it. What was *really* important? For others, a health scare, the death of a parent, caretaking an elderly parent, a child's problem at school, being laid off, or something innocuous . . . simply a moment in time that calls into question values and meaning . . . forces them, or forces us, to look at whether the path we are on is really the one we want to stay on.

Is it a midlife crisis? Not really, though very often midlife or mid-career, when we are going full-tilt with all the pressures, we are forced to examine what it all means. Regardless of when or why it happens, this sense of urgency, "The Urgency Factor" as we call it, has many people questioning: "Is that all there is?"

The Urgency Factor

What is The Urgency Factor? Look at how we live life nowadays. How many of us are wired and high-teched to distraction? Fifteen years ago, few of us had cellphones. Now we can't go to the local video store without calling home to our spouse or significant other with the movie selection. In fact, as more municipalities passed ordinances banning talking on cellphones while driving, what was the logical next step? It wasn't to understand that driving takes our full attention or to understand this can be dangerous and simply concentrate on the road. No, many people ran out and got hands-free cellphones.

And email. We're getting and sending emails at hours when it would be inappropriate to make a business call. After 9:00 at night, after 11:00 at night, and sometimes even on weekends. We're guilty of working to the wee hours, too.

But, in the end, what is so urgent? Why do we feel we have to be wired 24/7? What is it that can't wait until tomorrow? Why do we put our technology before our families and before ourselves? We've taken this trend for granted, without questioning how it is throwing our lives out of balance. It's causing some of the rooms in our house to become so large as to threaten the very *foundation* of our houses—and these rooms take away from the rooms that *should* be bigger.

Getting Back in Balance

A house is never going to be divided into 8 or 10 perfectly even rooms. Think about your dream home, whether that's where you reside right now or not. Your dream home may have a "great room," that supersized living area. It may have smaller rooms, like a cozy den, or a smaller guest bedroom. The master bedroom may be large enough to include a seating area. In any case, you won't find a house with every room the same size.

Ideally, however, the house, when looked at as a whole, will be pleasing. To borrow from the ancient art of feng shui, it will have balance and serenity. It will be a place worth coming home to at night. It won't be so out of balance that it topples on the foundation. The foundation will be firm, strong, and architecturally sound. If you're like most of us, your dream house, this metaphor we're using for life, doesn't look that way now. And even if you take all the suggestions in this book, you have to realize that at times life will simply happen. In other words, your life may come out of balance at tax time, or maybe you will have a parent who falls ill, or you may have a health scare. For Erica, a recent surgery meant the entire house was consumed with health. For Kathy, dealing with an aging parent meant there was little time for writing. It's okay to find yourself out of balance at times. What's not okay is watching a year go by without making the kind of significant life changes that will bring you a greater sense of balance. Everything can't be urgent all of the time.

Examining the problem is the first step toward remodeling your life and your house. Now that you have taken a hard look at whether or not your life is in balance, it's time to move on to each of the areas and overhaul and then fine-tune your life so that your house looks more like this:

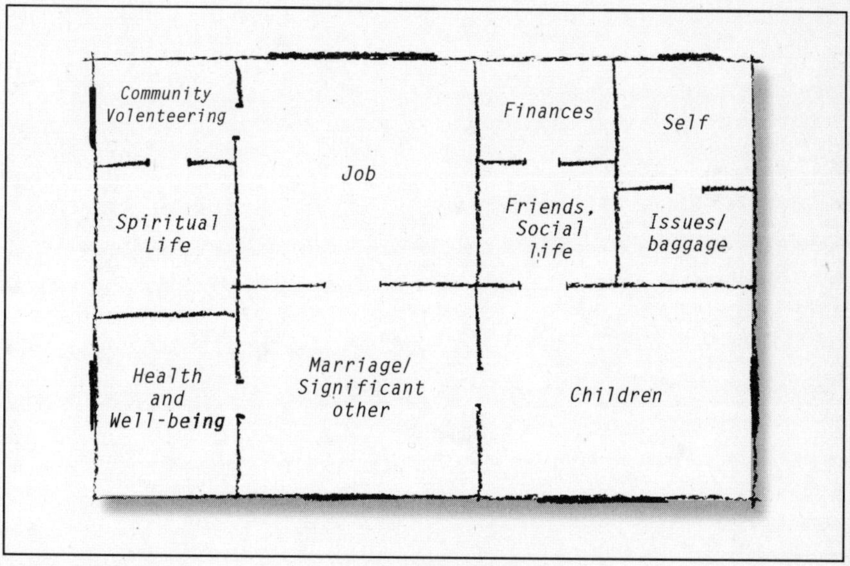

CHAPTER 2

IT'S TIME FOR A CHANGE

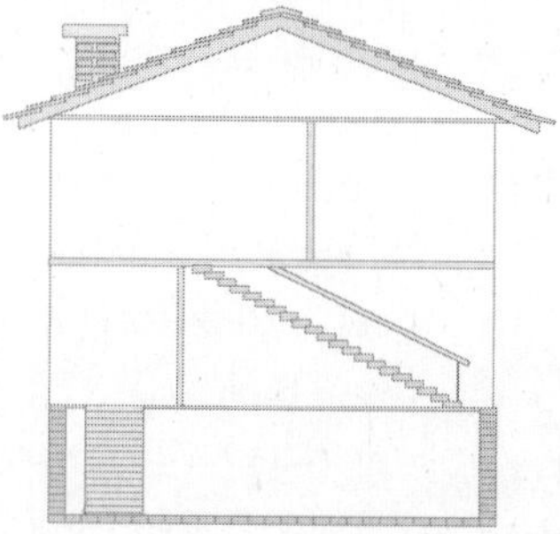

How often do you think about change? If you're anything like the rest of us, you think about change quite a bit. Many of us think about making changes in our career, relationships, or finances, but how many consider making a self-change? When life feels off-balance and out of sync, it's often because you've forgotten about yourself.

So many people get frustrated and give up when it comes to changing an aspect of their life. The most infamous example is the ill-fated New Year's resolution. Who hasn't made a few of those? As New Year's Eve draws near, everybody starts to at least think about making some kind of a resolution. Even the newspapers take reader polls and comment about it. Television reporters talk about it, "This year I am going to eat better and get in shape." Check back a month later and you'll find that most New Year's resolutions have been tossed on the shelf only to be resurrected again the next year.

Most resolutions are doomed right from the start. There are several reasons for failure, but the most important one is because there is no real plan in place for the change to occur. For example, when the television reporter comments that he would like to eat better, what *exactly* is his plan?

Does he even know? Is he going to start counting calories, eliminate fat from his diet, or fill his refrigerator with nothing but fruits and vegetables? Is he planning to do something even more extreme and become a raw food person? No plan means no map, and without a map, you simply don't know where you're going. The best intentions for change will fail when there is no plan to guide you along the way.

This book is all about change. This chapter focuses on self-change. Before we go any further, you are going to need a pencil and some paper. You may be thinking, "I know what I want to change, why do I have to write anything down?" Writing things down is the first step to building a plan. It is the first step toward taking action. Taking an idea out of your head and putting it on paper makes it all the more real.

Are We Happy Yet?

According to U.S. research, happiness is an elusive quality. In fact, the more comfortable life becomes, the more dissatisfied and discontented we are with it. The evidence indicates that a 25-year-old is four times more likely to be depressed today than in the 1950s. Professional men and women are the unhappiest of all (About.com).

An existing problem affects the balance we strive for in our lives. A lingering or developing concern makes everything else in your life feel worse. Anyone who has ever experienced money problems knows exactly what we mean. When money is tight or when credit card companies are calling your house at dinnertime, the tension spills over into your relationships, the job, and your outlook on life. Financial stress can feel as if you're drowning under the roar of pounding waves. It seems as if each time you try to climb out, another wave knocks you under. It can feel as if your life is coming apart.

The first move toward change in anyone's life is to take an inventory of what's working and what's not. When you are stressed, it's easy to conclude that everything is going wrong. Inside your mind it feels like the *War of the Worlds.* That's what makes getting thoughts down on paper helpful. Often when you get your concerns out of your head and down on paper, you discover there's more going on in your world that's right than wrong. It's not unusual for one or two issues to make your life seem as if there is no balance.

What about yourself is going well? What aspects of yourself do you perceive as healthy and strong?

1 ____

2 ____

3 ____

4 ____

5 ____

On the flip side, what aspects of yourself would you like to change? What are the concerns that wear you down?

1 ____

2 ____

3 ____

4 ____

5 ____

Throughout this book you will hear us talk about "fuzzy thinking" versus "clear thinking." Fuzzy thinking puts you on the fast track for failing. You have a few ideas in your head, but you have never gotten them down on paper. That's no different than driving your car in the fog. You sort of know the road in front of you, but you can't be positive. Keep in mind that the more specific you are in listing your goals, the better you'll be able to watch and monitor your progress. Here is an example of fuzzy and clear thinking:

Instead of Fuzzy Thinking	Think Clearly
I am going to start eating better. →	I am going to add fruit and vegetables to my daily diet. I am going to stop eating fast food. I am going to keep a food journal and observe what I am really eating in a week.

(continued)

Instead of Fuzzy Thinking	Think Clearly
I am going to get my house organized. →	I am going to make a list of every thing that needs to be done in my house and prioritize the things that should be done first. I am going to set aside some time this week and do the first thing on my list.
I am going to start saving some money. →	I am going to have money automatically withdrawn from my paycheck into a savings account. I am going to make an appointment with an accountant or financial planner this week.
I am going to start doing more with my family. →	I am going to call a family meeting and find out what we can all enjoy together. I am going to declare one Sunday a month as Family Day—no chores, no errands.
I want to change jobs. →	I am going to update my resume. I am going to make a list of strong job leads. I am going to practice my job interview skills.

Spinning Wheels

Since forever and a day, you have all had it drummed into you that to change your behavior, you must first understand why you do what you do. To that we say, "Baloney." Understanding why you overeat, procrastinate, or spend too much money doesn't help you to solve those problems. As a matter of fact, all that you've gained is a better understanding of how you understand the problem.

Here Is an Example of What We Mean

Imagine for a moment that you have a fear of dogs. Just the sight of a big dog brings on a panic attack. Your fear of dogs goes back to childhood when the neighbor's German shepherd tried to take a chunk out of your thigh when you were seven years old.

Our Question to You

How does knowing the root of your fear of dogs help you to overcome your fear?

Erica and I have a friend that we like to call the Diva because she looks and acts like, well, a diva. The Diva is terrified of flying. She is an aviophobic, or someone who has a fear of flying. The Diva is so afraid to fly that she even hopes that there'll be a plane crash before she has to fly. In her phobic mind, a plane crash will statistically lessen the chances that her own plane will go down. The Diva never travels without her Valium, which she will take before, during, and after a flight. It is an absolute necessity that she has an aisle seat in the bowels of the plane. The very last row is ideal. The Diva figures that the survival rate in a crash is better in the back than in the front. "Everybody gets it in the front," she'll confide. Sitting in the middle seat will only bring on a claustrophobia attack. Likewise, looking out the window at 30,000 feet will kick-start her acrophobia, or fear of heights. Once her seat belt is securely fastened, the Diva flags down a flight attendant and orders a cocktail.

Our friend, the Diva, knows better than most why she has these phobias. Her fears are triggered by traumatic events from childhood stored in her memory. Unfortunately, her understanding of those events does not give her a single clue as to how she might overcome her phobic problems. The Diva has been to therapy, but all that she has gained is a better understanding of the trauma and how that has influenced her life. Knowing the root cause of her fears does not solve her fear of flying, fear of small spaces, or fear of heights. Even with all her analysis and years on the couch, the Diva has no idea how to control or overcome her many fears.

There are many mental health professionals trained and prepared to tell you why you do the things you do. Most are well-trained and dedicated professionals who handle difficult and often tragic cases. As in all professions, there are others in the field who are not as credible and who unwittingly do people a disservice.

A few years back, a friend of Kathy's walked into her office and announced, "Last night at my Overeaters Anonymous group I learned that I had a symbiotic relationship with food." She looked elated. Emily had been morbidly obese for years and desperately wanted to lose the weight. At nearly 400 pounds, Emily's medical problems were starting to become serious. She had high blood pressure, a sleep disorder, chronic back and joint aches, and the early stages of diabetes. Emily knew that she was shortening her life every year that she was obese. But a symbiotic relationship with food? That's not possible. In the depths of the ocean, the shark and the Remora fish share a symbiotic relationship. The Remora fish lives a blissful life riding the hydrodynamic bow wake of this feared ocean predator. In exchange for safety and all the food scraps it needs, the Remora fish picks clean debris and parasites from the shark's body. Both sea creatures share a mutually beneficial relationship.

Kathy looked at her friend and asked, "I understand what you get from food, but what does the food get from you?" Emily's face dropped as she realized the silliness in her announcement. "Not only that, Emily, how does knowing that help you to get your diet under control?"

Insight about your past or the problems in your life doesn't provide you with a guide on how to change. In this chapter, as in the chapters to follow, we are going to discuss making positive and successful changes in your life. It's not always easy, because important changes seldom are, but it is doable.

Write Your Own Map

When it comes to change, it's easy to think about what you don't want in your life as opposed to what you want. If asked, a good number of us might say, "I don't want to be fat" or "I don't want to procrastinate anymore." We are quick to be negative about ourselves.

Take a moment and consider what you want for yourself. As tempting as it is, try to avoid any escapades into magical thinking. Unless you're a nationally ranked tennis player, save your dreams of the U.S. Open for another day. Right now, it's time to restore the balance in your life.

What are your personal goals? (Remember to be clear and measurable.) If you could change anything right now, what would it be?

1 ______________________________

2 ______________________________

3 ______________________________

4 ______________________________

5 ______________________________

This next part is important. Imagine for a moment that you have accomplished everything on your personal self-list. Answer this question:

What will your life be like when these self-changes are behind you? What will you be doing that you're not doing right now?

1 ______________________________

2 ______________________________

3 ______________________________

4 ______________________________

5 ______________________________

Lastly, think for another moment and consider this question. This question is important because it's the first mile-marker you're going to see as you gain greater satisfaction in your self.

What will be the smallest sign that you are moving in the right direction and that you are moving away from the aspects of your life that have frustrated or slowed you down?

____

____

____

Throughout the chapters that follow, you will be asked to think small. The most ambitious plans fail because they were just that—ambitious. Small steps are manageable and easier to track. A small step is like a domino, when one starts to happen the rest will follow behind.

Too Big	Just Right
I'm going to write a best-selling novel.→	I am going to join a writers' group.
I'm going to run in the Boston Marathon. →	I am going to jog three times this week.
I'm going to become fluent in Spanish. →	I am going to enroll in a language class.
I'm going to stop procrastinating. →	I am going to make a list of things to do and commit to doing one thing each day.

There is a reward for taking tiny, realistic steps instead of giant leaps. The reward is that you will get to feel successful and have a sense of accomplishment. Instead of that haunting voice moaning in your head, "Yeah, I'm going to get to that this week," you can say, "I did it." The first makes you feel burdened while the second empowers you. If you can do that one small step, you can do the next, and so on.

Are You Missing from Your Life?

How is it possible that with more wealth, conveniences, and recreational time, we seem to be more unhappy than ever before? The changes to our lifestyle in this century have been spectacular. We are living longer with the help of medical and technological advances. Disposable income is up four-fold since the 1950s. Shopping has become as American as baseball. So how do you fit into this picture?

Consider how life was 100 years ago in 1904 and compare it to how we are living today:

- The average life expectancy in the United States was 47.
- There were only 8,000 cars in the United States and only 144 miles of paved road.
- The average U.S. worker made between $200 and $400 per year.
- There was no Mother's Day or Father's Day.
- Canned beer and iced tea hadn't been invented.
- The longest film was just 12 minutes.
- It took 52 days to travel by automobile from San Francisco to New York.

As compared to 2004:

- The average life expectancy in the United States is 79.
- There are over 132,432,000 registered automobiles in the United States.
- The U.S personal income per capita is $30,511.
- The average household has 2.4 television sets.
- Over 56.5 percent of U.S households have at least one computer.
- Over 50.5 percent of U.S. households have Internet access.
- You can get from New York to San Francisco in less than five hours with a good tailwind.

It may be the reason so many of us feel unhappy is because we're working like mad trying to get "ahead." Although we have a vague notion of what life will be like when we get to this destination known universally as "ahead," we keep pushing on. Like some hedonistic treadmill in which we strive to have a bigger home or a better car, we don't stay satisfied for long. After a while, it's back on the treadmill for the quest to get more stuff. Perhaps we are all guilty of thinking, "If a little is good, more is better." Somewhere on the treadmill we lose ourselves.

OUTSIDE THE BOX

Kathy—If a psychic told me that at age 44 I was going to become involved in martial arts, I probably would have asked for my money back. At that point I was the executive chauffeur not only for my kids, but for my mother as well. A typical day meant that I would be driving anywhere from three to five hours a day in addition to work, taking care of the house, doing a zillion errands, making dinner, and last but not least, helping with homework. I was exhausted and running ragged. I even looked half-crazed. I was on the bottom of my own "to-do" list. A trip to the doctor revealed for the first time that my blood pressure was elevated. That got my attention, but I still didn't have a plan. One night when I was picking up my kids from karate I lingered long enough to catch a glimpse of an adult class. At that moment the light went back on in my darkened brain. I was mesmerized by the energy of the master instructor. He was an older man but he moved with the grace and power of a Barishnikov. What's more, the students that were jumping and kicking through the air were my own age. I signed my husband and I up the next day. For the first time in a long while, I feel healthy. We've made good friends. At a time when everyone is caught in car pool hell, we do something unusual. We go as a family.

Erica—I have a few friends with whom I would like to socialize, but these women place themselves last on their own list. They say they can't possibly go to a movie—their husbands won't "let them." And even if they were "allowed," they couldn't take away time from their kids. I love my children, but frankly, I also love myself. It is not selfish to take time to read, to go out to the movies, or to do other things that refresh my batteries. I am as busy as the next parent, but I am not last on my own list.

On a scale ranging from 1 to 10, with 1 being "the worst" and 10 being "great," how well would you say you are taking care of yourself right now?

How have you managed to maintain your self-happiness so far? What is working for you?

What could you do to bring your score up half a notch, say to a 9 ½? If you gave yourself a 10, what can you continue to do to keep your score at a 10?

What kinds of things have you been doing to keep your score at a two or a five? Think about it—you didn't give yourself a zero, so you must be doing a few things correctly. What have you managed to do right?

What is one more thing you can do to find balance in yourself and bring your score up a point?

What will you do to ensure that you keep doing that one small thing?

How will your life be different when you manage to get your score up a few points?

What will you be doing that you are not doing now?

Who will be the most surprised about these changes in you?

Think Like a Kid

Have you ever noticed how kids view the world? They seem to notice all the things that we as adults take for granted. Walk the beach with children and you'll be stopping every few seconds to watch a sand crab, pick up shells, or stare at the colors in a jellyfish. Twisted knots of seaweed hide strange bits of treasure. Every step along the beach leads to a new adventure, a new possibility.

It's different when adults walk the beach. Your mind is wrapped up by life concerns—your relationship with your mother, that impending lawsuit, and your kids' school tuition. You seldom, if ever, look down to see where you are going. Where are your possibilities?

Take some time and use the template in this chapter and the ones that follow to create new possibilities for yourself. Look at the world with a child's eye and take a chance to do something for yourself. No matter how small your first step might be, it is a step nonetheless. Like the acrobat who takes that first tentative step onto the wire, put one step in front of the other, and don't look back.

CHAPTER 3

A BLUEPRINT FOR FINANCIAL BALANCE

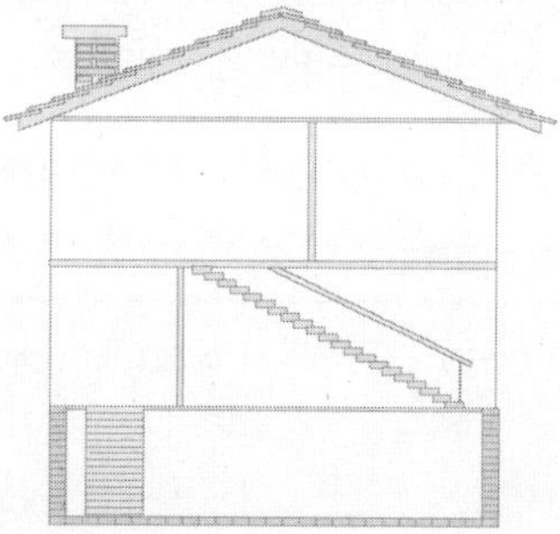

Psychologists have always said that public speaking is the most universal fear. We're not so convinced. In fact, few situations can get the heart racing, the stomach knotting, or the palms sweating like financial trouble. A good many of us stick our heads in the sand like an ostrich when we get into hot water with money. The bills start to pile up—first on the kitchen counter and later in a box in the back of a closet. When the collection agencies start calling you at all hours, you're grateful to have Caller ID.

A marriage can disintegrate under financial strain. In fact, studies indicate that financial disagreement is one of the leading causes of marital problems. Who can relax and enjoy one another when you're worried about paying for your kids' school and the mortgage?

Basically, when it comes to money, it all boils down to this—we spend too much and save too little. You aren't the first person to scratch your head wondering, "How can I make this much and have so little to show for it?" A Saturday matinee with two children will cost you nearly $30, even before you head to the snack counter for sodas and popcorn.

The fear of money and financial stress robs you of confidence. After a while you can start to feel as if the situation is hopeless and you'll never get it together. But it doesn't have to be that way. It's time to change the way you view yourself in relation to money. It's time to take back your power over money. If that sounds like magical thinking, you are wrong.

Stop right here and go get a pencil and a pad of paper because in this chapter you're going to need it. To get your financial house in order you have to look your money concerns straight in the eye. You also need to know what you want. You might say, "That's simple, I don't want financial problems anymore." But that's fuzzy thinking and not clear thinking. Be more specific. To get to where you want to go you need to know where you're going. The more specific you are in listing your goals, the better you'll be able to know if you're making progress. Think of your goals as mile markers.

Instead of Fuzzy Thinking	**Think Clearly**
I don't want any more money pressures →	I want to eliminate my credit card debt.
	I want to pay my bills on time.
	I want to put money into my savings account each week.
	I want to buy a house.
	I want to start saving for my retirement.

Write Your Own Map

Think for a moment and imagine yourself exactly where you want to be financially. If you can, resist the impulse to imagine that you're a Power Ball winner and have more money than you can spend in 10 lifetimes. If you do happen to win the lottery one day that's fantastic, but for the time being keep your feet firmly planted on the ground.

What are your financial goals? What financial difficulties would you like to resolve?

1 ____________________

2 ____________________

3 ____________________

4 ____

5 ____

This next part is important. Imagine for a moment that you have accomplished everything on your financial list. Answer this question:

What will your life be like when these financial concerns are behind you? What will you be doing?

____

____

____

____

____

____

Finally, think for another moment and answer this question. This question is important because it's the first mile marker you're going to see as you take yourself to a better financial life.

What will be the smallest sign that you are moving in the right direction and that you are moving away from financial stress?

____

____

A small sign is exactly that—small. Don't be concerned that your sign seems too small. When you start to create one small change, other changes will follow. When there is a positive change in one area, other positive changes will occur somewhere else. So think small, no matter how unimportant it may seem and how far you may feel from your goals.

Too Big	**Just Right**
I'll take a vacation. →	This week I will put $50 dollars toward a vacation.

Too Big	Just Right
I'll cut up all my credit cards. →	I will put all my credit cards away except for one.
I'll pay off my credit cards. →	Today I will pay cash when I go to the store.

It really is a good idea to start with small signs. If a sign is too big, the chances are that you will feel overwhelmed. Doctors will tell you that if you want to lose weight and keep it off, the best thing is to lose just one to two pounds a week. Studies show that people who stay to that recommendation keep the weight off. Those who lost a large amount of weight too fast not only gained all their weight back but also put more on. The same thing is true when noticing small signs of change. Those who take small, baby steps to their goal tend to be successful whereas those who take on too much too fast may fail.

Stop Counting Other People's Money

Money trouble feels lonely. You're convinced that everyone must be in better financial shape than you. The world seems to be dancing by without a care in the world, but not you. Friends and neighbors renovate their kitchens, take the kids to Disney World, and buy big-screen plasma televisions.

If you think you're adrift on a slab of ice all alone, think again. You are not as alone as you think. We may all have been fooled into believing that everyone is much better off financially than they actually are. According to the Federal Reserve Board, paying down debt accounts for 14.3% of take-home pay, the highest rate since 1986. Wait—there's more. The Mortgage Bankers Association of America states that in the last quarter of 2000, mortgage delinquencies rose to 4.5%—the highest delinquency rate since 1992.

Family Income Levels

2001	Personal income per capita	$30,511
2000	Median four-person family income	$65,381
2001	Consumer credit outstanding	$1,702.8 billion

Feeling a little less lonely? You should because many people are struggling just as much as you. Remember, the grass always looks greener on the other side. How many times have you found yourself thinking, "How can they afford that ski vacation every winter?" The truth is that they probably can't afford it any more than you can. Although they may not have the cash to pay for it, they do have something else—credit cards.

Credit Cards Can Be Hazardous to Your Financial Health

How did we ever survive before credit cards? They are so seductively easy. You don't need to worry about carrying cash. You can purchase items even if you only have a dollar left in your checking account. You can deal with that problem when the credit card statement arrives in the mail. The other great aspect of having a credit card is that you can take your time paying down your balance. The credit card company will be more than happy to let you make minimum payments as long as you also pay their 23 percent finance charge along with it.

Facing the Truth about Your Credit Cards

Name of Credit Card	Amount Owed	Annual Interest Rate	Minimum Monthly Payment	Actual Payment
Total Number of Credit Cards	Total Amount Owed			Total Amount You Pay per Month

If you're carrying a large balance on your credit cards you may want to consider consolidating with a lower interest credit card or home equity loan. There are credit card companies that will allow you to merge all of your debt onto one credit card, which is a sensible thing to do if you find yourself paying down credit cards with interest rates at over 14%. Ask yourself what makes more sense—paying a $7,000 balance at 13% interest or 21%? What's worse is if you've been making only the minimum monthly payment on your credit card debt. What typically happens is that you end up paying only the finance charge and never the actual balance. It's like rolling down the window of your car and throwing the money out.

Another way to go if you have a large credit card balance is to apply for a home equity loan. You do, however, have to be a homeowner. Not only will you save money in interest payments but also in federal income taxes, because the home equity interest is tax-deductible.

Here are a few suggestions to help keep your toes away from the credit card flames:

1. *Limit your number of credit cards*. Ask yourself this question, "How many credit cards do I really need?" Is it necessary for you to have a credit card for every major department store, discount store, gas station, and home improvement center? Some of us are walking around with 15 or 20 credit cards in our wallets and all those cards have balances. A smart piece of advice is simply to get rid of most of these cards. Limit yourself to one or maybe two major credit cards that charge the lowest interest rate and cut the rest up with a scissor.
2. *Start to use a debit card*. Unfortunately, we have become a credit card society. Without a credit card you could find yourself out of luck when it comes to renting a car or making airline reservations. Debit cards offer the best of both worlds. Debit cards give you the convenience of a credit card in that you can use them most everywhere. In fact, most debit cards look just like a credit card with a MasterCard or Visa logo. The important difference between a debit card and a credit card is that purchases are automatically withdrawn from your checking account. As handy as debit cards are, it is important to know that unlike credit cards,

debit cards are not protected against fraud like traditional credit cards.

3. *Contact your bank to request that your credit card limit be capped.* The psychology behind credit card companies is clever. They "reward" active cardholders by raising their credit limit. The cardholder thinks, "Gee, they really like me. They're letting me spend more." Here's the thing: just because you've been given a higher credit limit doesn't mean you have to accept it. In fact, you can refuse the increase or better yet, call all your credit card companies and have them lower the limit on each of your cards.

4. *Switch from a credit card to a charge card*. While a credit card allows you to make payments on a balance, a charge card, such as American Express, requires that you pay off your balance in full at the end of the month. The advantage to a charge card is that you won't be carrying a balance and growing finance fees. The only disadvantage is if you've over spent and can't afford to pay the bill at the end of the month.

5. *Resist the temptation to open a charge account in a department store just to get the initial purchase discount*. How many times have you been approached at the counter of a retail store and offered to open a charge account? The sales clerk sweetens the deal by offering an additional 10 or 15% discount on all purchases that day. However, the interest rates on department store cards are typically over 20%. If you already have an American Express, Visa, or MasterCard, there is no reason to add more plastic to your wallet.

6. *Resist, resist, resist*. Credit card companies are very clever at persuading consumers into spending more money. One of their telemarketers catches you off guard at home and the next thing you know, you're getting a new microwave plus a magazine subscription to *Pet World*.

7. *Practice the following line over and over until you have it memorized*: *"No thank you. Have a nice day—bye."* The next time a telemarketer calls to offer you a new credit card plus a trip to Great Adventures Theme Park, hang up the telephone. Don't feel guilty

about it. You are just one person on a list of possibly hundreds who will be called that day. When you hang up the telemarketer says, "Next."

Credit Card Reports and Ratings

Your credit history begins the moment you obtain approval on your first application. Perhaps it was your first car loan or credit card, or maybe a school loan.

The best way to obtain and keep a good credit rating is to pay back the money you owe on time. When you make late payments or fail to pay something back, the credit card bureau labels you as a credit risk. The fact that you are a risk will rear its head each time you attempt to get a credit card, borrow money, purchase a car, or get a mortgage.

The disturbing thing is that a bad credit rating stays in your credit history for seven years. This can happen if you miss a payment or even if you are just late with a payment.

Your local credit bureau updates your credit report each month by contacting your creditors. Creditors not only include banks and credit cards, but also utilities, landlords, and even hospitals. The bureau collects data on whether or not you pay bills and loans on time, whether or not you miss payments, and your current credit rating with that creditor. The data collected is filed in your credit history and will rear its head each time you apply for something.

What you should be aware of is that credit bureaus do make mistakes. That's why it is a good idea to get a copy of your credit report. Once you get it, review it carefully. If you find a mistake, which is certainly possible, contact the creditor who filed the report to the credit bureau and ask them to have the information corrected.

You can do that by contacting:

- Equifax: 800-685-1111 or www.equifax.com
- Experian: 800-397-3742 or www.experian.com
- TransUnion: 800-888-4213 or www.tuc.com

OUTSIDE THE BOX

Kathy—My husband and I lived in Boca Raton, Florida for 12 years before returning to New York. We always joked that there must be a ghost living in our house because things were always disappearing. It seemed like if you put something down one moment, it was gone in the next. Whenever something disappeared, we'd say, "The ghost must have taken it." One day a very large check disappeared off the kitchen counter. We were frantic and ripped the house apart looking for it. Six months later I found it inside a dog food catalog in my laundry room. The ghost must have been planning to buy a few rawhide bones. Finally, it hit me. There was no ghost—we were disorganized from being spread too thin. We couldn't keep up with our schedules and the result was internal chaos. There is just one thing I can't figure out to this day. How did my gold locket get inside a picture frame in my living room? Hmm.

Erica—Please . . . finances and taxes are my two least favorite subjects. In fact, I am dizzy just thinking about writing about them. Recognizing this, I suggest that if you are equally phobic, get a sense of balance here by hiring a good bookkeeper or accountant. With this load off your shoulders, and you in more of a supervisory role going over the numbers, you divert your energies elsewhere.

Digging Out

It's often not easy to face, but before you can take steps to get out of debt you first must know how much you owe. Taking wild guesses at how much you owe isn't the best plan because some debts, such as credit cards, include late fees and interest charges. The best route is to lay all your debt down in front of you. Know what you owe. Only then can you make steps to dig out.

There are three important points to remember when you are trying to settle your money problems. You need to:

- ▲ Calculate how much you owe
- ▲ Determine how you got into debt
- ▲ Set a plan for getting out of debt

If you have found yourself with unmanageable debt, it is critical to your recovery to know how you got there in the first place. Not everyone lands in debt the same way. While overspending can cause debt, it can also be caused by job loss, illness, or a failed business. And another thing—not all debt is bad. In fact, there is good debt and bad debt.

Bad debt refers to such items as car loans, credit cards, or borrowing money to take vacations. These are things you consume, pay high interest rates on, and will never see again. On the other hand, borrowing money to purchase land or real estate is considered good debt because you can expect a return for your investment. Taking a loan to pay for a college education is also considered good debt.

Use the following worksheet to list all your debts. The worksheet is divided by categories: auto, credit cards, home, miscellaneous, and taxes. The items listed with an asterisk reflect items considered to be bad debt. At the end of this worksheet you will be able to compare your good versus bad debt. Total your debt by category, and then tabulate your grand total.

***Auto**

Loan, car #1	$____________
Loan, car #2	$____________
Total Auto Debt	$____________

***Credit Cards**

American Express	$____________
MasterCard	$____________
Visa	$____________

Discover	$__________
Store card #1	$__________
Store card #2	$__________
Store card #3	$__________
Total Credit Card Debt	$__________
Home	
Mortgage	$__________
*Appliances, installment plans	$__________
*Furniture, installment plans	$__________
Home equity loan	$__________
Utility bills (past due)	$__________
Total Home Debt	$__________
Miscellaneous	
Medical bills	$__________
*Personal loans	$__________
Student loans	$__________
Other loans	$__________
Total Miscellaneous Debt	$__________
Taxes	
Federal	$__________
State	$__________
Other	$__________
Total Tax Debt	$__________
Total of All Debts	$__________
Total Bad Debt	$__________
Total Good Debt	$__________

In this worksheet, we didn't include such routine expenses as current utility bills, food, and entertainment because living expenses are not part of your debt. However, your monthly costs do influence how much money you will have to pay down your debt.

Too Much of a Bad Thing

Setting a plan for getting debt under control includes knowing how much of your monthly income or take home pay is needed to pay it down.

- Tally up your monthly bad debt costs and for now, exclude the good debt. For example, suppose you earn $45,000 per year. A tally of your bad debt, such as car loans, credit cards, and personal loans, amounts to $15,000 of debt. Your bad debt is 33% of your total income.
- The formula looks like this:

$$\frac{\text{Debt}}{\text{Annual Income}} \times 100 = \text{Bad Debt Ratio}$$

$$\frac{\$15{,}000}{\$45{,}000} \times 100 = 33\%$$

Financial experts recommend that you keep bad debt below the 20% level. The higher this percentage, the greater the potential for your debt to grow and get out of control. You could be spreading yourself too thin and finding it harder and harder to keep up with monthly payments.

By now, you may be wondering how in the world did you get in such financial straits. As bad as you may feel, you took an important step by facing the debt and calculating how that amount impacts your salary. Now it's time to start digging.

- *Cut back on your unnecessary expenses*. This means eliminating or cutting back wherever you can on such things as club memberships, the gym, cable TV, magazine and newspaper subscriptions, video rentals, pedicures, and dinners out until you are financially stable.

- *Put your credit cards away and use either cash or a debit card*. Remember that credit cards helped you to get into this mess in the first place.
- *Go for the biggest debts first*. Start paying down the credit cards with the largest balances because of their high interest rates. The longer these debts exist, the bigger they will grow.
- *Consider getting a consolidation loan*. Getting a consolidation loan from the bank can help decrease the amount of money you are spending on interest payments. The catch here is to be disciplined enough to not start spending with your credit cards all over again.
- *Put something into your savings before you spend*. Get into the habit of putting money into your savings each week no matter how little it is. You will be amazed at how fast that amount grows. Better yet, arrange to have the money withdrawn from your paycheck and you will never miss it.

Taking Back Your Financial Life

It might surprise you to learn just how many people live paycheck to paycheck with little or nothing in a savings account. More alarming is how few people are saving for their retirement. Studies indicate that fewer than 20% of "Baby Boomers" are saving enough for their retirement. That means that a whopping 80% are going to be in a world of trouble come retirement.

You don't have to be on that wagon. Starting today you can do something different and begin to get your financial house in order. Sure, it may involve cutting back on your lifestyle, but think of the peace of mind you will have knowing that you are saving your money.

Before we ask you to reach for a pencil again, here are a few savings ideas that may help you:

- *Save your money before you get the chance to get your hands on it*. A very effective way to save money is to have it automatically withdrawn from your paycheck. That way you don't even have to think about it. Your money can be withdrawn and put into a U.S. savings bond payroll deduction plan or even mutual funds.

- ▲ *Look around to see where you can cut back*. It may seem insignificant, but even seemingly small expenses can add up over the course of a year. For instance, the home delivery of newspapers. If you find that you're throwing away more newspapers than you actually read, then perhaps you should cancel your subscription. Buy the paper when you have time to read it. The average home-delivered newspaper costs around $60 per month. That's $720 in savings over the course of a year. Do you have a membership to a gym but never go? Cancel it.
- ▲ *Put your annual raise or year-end bonus away.* Take the money you receive from a bonus or a raise and start a retirement or college fund. Consider it "found" money.
- ▲ *Pay in cash whenever you can*. When you reach for cash instead of a credit card the chances are that you will spend less. Paying in cash means no ongoing credit card balances and no finance charges.
- ▲ *Pay off high-rate debts first*. Pay down first any debt that carries a high interest rate such as credit cards and car loans. The longer you carry this debt, the more interest you will pay. As we mentioned earlier, consider obtaining a home equity loan to pay off large credit balances.
- ▲ *Free is good*. Why should you be paying for checking accounts when some banks offer free checking? You don't have to pay for checking, nor should you. Some credit card companies charge annual fees as high as $300 a year. Look for credit cards that offer no annual fees.

It's time to write down your financial goals. You may be asking, why should I write them down? I want to save money—period. Remember in the beginning of this chapter when we talked about fuzzy versus clear thinking? Saying that you want to save money is another example of fuzzy thinking. You can't get an active plan in gear with your head full of murky thoughts. Knowing what you want in clear terms sets the stage for success. Writing goals down on paper makes them more real, and things look different on paper. You need to be able to recognize the signs or mile markers that you are moving in the right direction.

Fuzzy Thinking	Clear Thinking
I want to save money from my paycheck.→	I will use automatic withdrawal to take $150 from my paycheck and place it into a savings account.

Write down your top five financial goals.

1. ______________________________
2. ______________________________
3. ______________________________
4. ______________________________
5. ______________________________

Now ask yourself this question:

On a scale ranging from 1 to 10, with 1 being "the worst" and 10 being "great," how well would you say you are saving your money right now?

____

____

If you answered with a 9 or 10, that's impressive. But stick around because there is always more to learn. Remember that life has a way of throwing you a curve ball just when you think you have it all together. There are always unexpected babies, job changes, divorce, home renovations, and other events that can affect your financial balance. It's always wise to keep your financial muscles well-toned. If your score was as high as a 9 or 10 then ask yourself this question:

How have you managed to be so resourceful with your money?

____

____

____

What could you do to bring your score up half a notch, say to a 9½? If you gave yourself a 10, what can you continue to do to keep your score at a 10?

____

____

____

____

Many of us wouldn't give ourselves a high score when it comes to saving money. In fact, many would score themselves lower than they actually should. What score did you give yourself? A two? Three? Five?

Ask yourself this question:

What kinds of things have you been doing to keep your score at a two or five? Think about it—you didn't give yourself a zero so you must be doing a few things correctly. What have you managed to do right?

____

____

____

____

If you are thinking that there simply couldn't be anything in a score that low, you're wrong. If you didn't give yourself a flat zero it is because in some small ways you are doing a few positive things to save your money. It may feel small or inconsequential but change is built on tiny, baby steps. A step in the right direction is powerful because it takes you closer to your goals.

What is one more thing you can do to save money and bring your score up a point?

____

____

____

What will do you do to ensure that you keep doing that one small thing?

____

____

How will your life be different when you manage to get your score up a few points?

____

____

What will you be doing that you are not doing now?

____

____

Who will be the most surprised about these financial changes?

____

____

____

Balance Your Emotional Budget

As we have laid it out here, finances aren't a big mystery. Debt is bad; savings are good. Planning for the future is even better. IRAs and saving for kids' college funds, however, can seem like a pipe dream if you can't get a handle on your spending and debt. It's important, then, to take a look at your emotional budget.

An emotional budget, and in turn balancing it, involves examining your *feelings* about money. For instance, if you look at a closet full of clothes and think you have "nothing" to wear and then, despite your debt, go out to buy new clothes, there is some emotional component to your spending. If you are tempted to buy a car, a set of golf clubs, or an expensive vacation and put it on credit because you feel like you "have" to have it, this is also an emotional button.

The key to an emotionally balanced budget is to "see it through." Before you go shopping, before you shop on e-Bay, purchase a vacation, or go out for that ultra-expensive dinner, see it through to the next step—the bill arriving. Ask yourself "Is this a *want* or a *need?*" If it is a want, examine where those feelings are coming from. If it is a need, ask yourself if this newly purchased item will solve your debt problems and make you feel better in the long run.

A true sense of balance will come when you have made strides in reducing your debt, saved for the future, and stopped living from paycheck to paycheck, and purchase to purchase.

CHAPTER 4

HEALTH AND WELL-BEING: FINDING AND KEEPING BALANCE

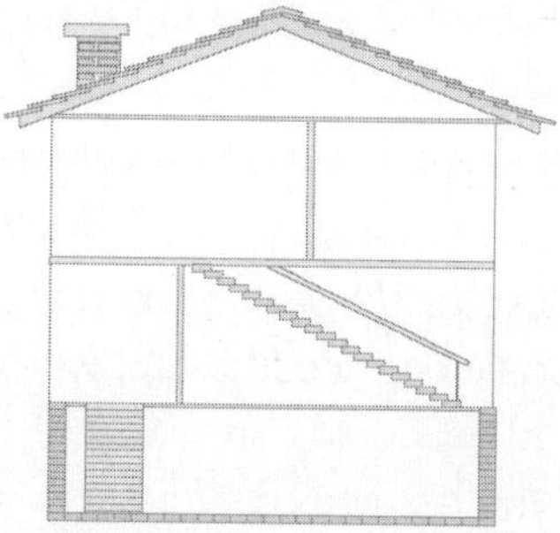

It happens to all of us, sooner or later. We wake up at age 30 or 35, 45 or 50, and we hear . . . what is that noise? It's the tell-tale popping of joints as we climb out of bed. Health and general well-being are one of the areas in life that tend to suddenly surprise us as being out of balance. And the surprise is all too unpleasant.

Here are some "surprises" that happen to all or most of us at some point or another:

- ▲ The numbers game: We go for a physical and are astonished to find our total cholesterol hovers near the 250 mark. How did that happen?
- ▲ We are invited to our 10-year, 20-year, or fill-in-the-blank-year reunion . . . and suddenly we are aware of a veritable smorgasbord of problems from not being able to squeeze into our tux or size-10 dress, to noticing we feel winded after climbing a flight of stairs.
- ▲ We ache. We're not talking about the occasional sprain or bruise. We're talking about waking up each day painfully aware of being out of shape, a bad back, or the creeping onset of arthritis.

- ▲ We stumble across an old photo of ourselves from when we ran track in college or when we were the star of the baseball team. We are painfully aware those days are long gone.
- ▲ Stress has become such a way of life for us that before we realize it, we have signs of stress overload, from heart palpitations to chronic forgetfulness.
- ▲ And worst of all, some readers of this book are going to face the sudden onset of a serious health problem. It won't be so "sudden" in actuality. Perhaps those arteries have been clogging up for a long time, but the serious consequences will spring on us in frightening fashion in the form of a heart attack or other serious health dilemma.

Whatever the catalyst for the realization that your health and general well-being are out of balance, heeding the warning signs is important. Sure, someone who is 40 years old may live to the ripe old age of 80, but we all know someone who has keeled over at his or her desk at 50. What if you only had months, not years to live? And what if you could change that forecast by taking back your health?

Using the same thinking we'll apply throughout the book, it isn't enough to say "I want to be as thin as I was in high school" (which is probably not a realistic or attainable goal) or "I want to be healthy." Instead, you have to take your fuzzy-thinking (which may have gotten you into trouble in the first place) and clarify it.

Instead of Fuzzy Thinking	Think Clearly
I don't want to be overweight anymore. →	I want to lose 20 pounds by Memorial Day weekend. I won't eat after 7:00 p.m.
I want to be in good physical shape. →	I want to make time in my schedule to work out three times a week. I will take the stairs at work and walk on my lunch hour. I will meet with a physical trainer and get an exercise regime that's right for me.

Instead of Fuzzy Thinking	Think Clearly
I don't want to be stressed out. →	I want to meditate every day, starting with 15 minutes a day. I want to find a half hour each day to relax with no phones, television, or other intrusions.

Write Your Own Map

Most of us know what we don't want to be: overweight, out of shape, so stressed our pulses race at that first telephone call of the day. But to find and restore balance, the clearer way to think involves creating your own map to balance. You can conquer your balance issues with a well-thought-out plan. So think about the areas of health and well-being that you would most like to change and define them here.

What are your health and wellness goals? (Remember to be specific and choose goals that are measurable.) What health problems would you like to resolve?

1 ______________________________

2 ______________________________

3 ______________________________

4 ______________________________

5 ______________________________

This next part is important. Imagine for a moment that you have accomplished everything on your wellness list. Answer this question:

What will your life be like when these wellness concerns are behind you? What will you be doing?

____

____

____

____

____

____

Now, as you ponder this, please also shut off any old negative "tapes." Remember, this is where you need to think positively. For instance, it's no use yelling internally to yourself that you "allowed" yourself to become 50 pounds overweight. Better to absorb what it will be like if you shed those unwanted pounds for good. Also, think of the big picture. If you shed 50 pounds, chances are the positive repercussions would translate into all areas of your life from self-confidence to your sexuality.

Finally, think for another moment and answer this question. This question is important because it's the first mile marker you're going to see as you take yourself to a better wellness life.

What will be the smallest sign that you are moving in the right direction and that you are moving away from stress/fatigue/unwellness?

____

____

As we just said, the repercussions of change can reverberate throughout your life. So while you may feel losing 10 pounds or making time to meditate each day is a very small step, it will likely impact you throughout your world. Let's use taking up yoga for instance. Sure it's the hottest trend from Madonna to Gwyneth Paltrow. It seems like everyone is doing it. But if you were to take up yoga twice a week, you would likely find, if you kept it up, that your sense of balance improved, your flexibility would greatly increase (you know . . . when you sit down cross-legged on the floor with your kids, you won't groan when you have to climb back up!), and your stress would drop. When there is a positive change in one area, other positive changes will occur somewhere else. So think small, no matter how unimportant it may seem, and how far you may feel from your goals.

Too Big	Just Right
I'll do yoga seven days a week and get in phenomenal shape, even though the last time I exercised was 1975. →	This week I will try two yoga classes offered at my gym.
I'll never allow another sweet to pass through my lips again. →	I'll start by giving up my nightly dish of ice cream on Mondays.
I'll lose 50 pounds and fit into my old prom dress. →	I realize I have had three children and my body has changed. I will aim to lose five pounds in the next month.

It really is a good idea to start with small signs. Also avoid all or nothing thinking. For instance, many people will say "I'll start a diet on Monday." They will eat healthily on Monday, and even Tuesday. On Wednesday, the department secretary is retiring after 30 years and the staff throws her a party. Before you know it, you've indulged in a little bit of every potluck offering at the buffet table. What will you do? For many, disgust and self-loathing will lead them to say "the hell with it . . . I can't do it . . . forget it" and go back to their old eating habits. This type of black and white thinking is the *opposite* of balance. Instead, think "I went off my diet today, but it was a lovely occasion. Tomorrow I will walk an extra 20 minutes and I'll get back on my regime." No self-loathing. Instead, it's about balance and moving on.

The Grass Isn't Always Greener

In the quest for balance, it does you no good to look at others and bemoan how your friend Sandy has the same size-three waist she had at her wedding, or your friend Sam can still run a mile in under four minutes. The most important person in the quest for balance is yourself.

If you can't resist looking around, don't concentrate solely on the "beautiful people." The box on page 44 has some sobering statistics about being overweight and obesity in America. When it comes to being out of shape or unwell, most of us have a lot of company.

Feeling a little less lonely? You should because many people are struggling just as much as you are. Remember, the grass always looks greener

Obesity in America

More than 60% of all U.S. adults are overweight, according to the Centers for Disease Control (CDC). A whopping 20% of Americans are considered obese, up from 12% in 1991. Sadly, the CDC says that obesity rates among children have reached "epidemic" proportions (Forbes.com, 11/20/02).

on the other side. How many times have you found yourself thinking, "How can she stay so thin?" or "How can he find time to jog every day?" In actuality, the people in question may have made a commitment to balance. Or they may be just as out of balance in some other area of their lives that just isn't visible to you. We'll never forget meeting a guy who was the picture of health. He ran every day and looked to be in extraordinary health. Of course, he also packed away a fifth of scotch every night. We still don't know how he managed to run every day, but he made his own pact with the devil!

The 24/7 Lifestyle May Be Hazardous to Your Health

We've talked about the 24/7 lifestyle and the urgency factor. Here are some classic signs that the frenetic pace of the technological age has helped to take you out of balance:

- ▲ Your lifestyle is so hectic, the only time you can return phone calls is via cell phone on your commute.
- ▲ You only manage to eat a "normal" dinner one night out of five during the week. The rest of the time, it's strictly high-fat take-out.
- ▲ You never sleep more than five or six hours a night because you are up late catching up on work or paying bills and organizing your personal life.
- ▲ You haven't taken a nonworking vacation in a number of years.
- ▲ The last time you consistently exercised, you did Jane Fonda aerobics tapes wearing leg warmers.
- ▲ Meals, family time, kids' soccer games, and quiet evenings at home, are all interrupted by work-related calls.

It's great to be dedicated to your job. The technological age has also given us the ability to dial up from home, from a cell phone, or in our hotel rooms when we're on the road—anywhere a satellite connection can be made. But if the reality is that there are only 24 hours in a day (which, we know, is shocking . . . we sometimes think we need a 36-hour day!) something has to give if life is lived entirely on the run.

Examine some of your out-of-balance signs in the 24/7 millennium:

1 ______________________________

2 ______________________________

3 ______________________________

4 ______________________________

5 ______________________________

Now, what small steps can you take to reduce this technological overload? Can you ban calls during the dinner hour? Can you decide that you won't check email after a certain hour? Can you reduce the number of nights you eat take-out in favor of more leisurely meals?

Stress: Don't Fight-or-Flight It Anymore

There's an expression: If you had no stress you'd be dead. What? You may ask. It's true. Stress is a part of life, and we have a million small stresses a day, and a thousand tiny annoyances. They're part of life, and stress keeps us safe. Stress is our lightning-fast reaction to swerve and avoid the truck that drifted into our lane. It tells us the shower temperature is too hot and we need to lower it. Stress reminds us, through tension in our bodies, to put on our best performance when we have to give a presentation. Stress can elevate our "game" in work and life to "the next level."

Stress, as most of us know, is triggered by our "fight or flight response" to the aggravations of daily life. When we were cave people, those who were attuned to running away from the saber-toothed tiger survived. Those that reacted too slowly to exhibit "flight" or were too weak to "fight" died and were unable to continue their genetic lineage. Over time, that fight or flight response became very fine-tuned indeed.

The problem is that most of us aren't running from a wooly mammoth. Instead, we're dealing with our teenagers' sullenness, the stress of confronting our boss over a raise, public speaking, or unbearable commutes. We are dealing with the stresses of urban life and feeling too crowded and technologically overloaded. Our bodies, however, don't know this. The same "fight or flight" chemicals that kept us alive as we dodged wild animals are now released when we have to stand in front of a crowd and present our marketing proposal. Our body reacts by sweating, shaking, and palpitating.

This gives some of us an edge. We train ourselves to take a deep breath and then we "nail it"—our performance is rock solid. The chemicals subside. We relax. The stress is over.

Increasingly, though, many of us have so much stress that those feelings and chemicals never subside. We're so stressed we wander around in a state of hyperalertness. The constant release of these stress chemicals impacts our immune system, our sense of sanity, and our well-being—our health.

The bigger problem is that we can't necessarily get rid of what is stressing us.

That's right. It would be lovely if, in our book on balance, we could say, "Go out and win the lottery and live the rest of your life being pampered and catered to." But we can't. And we also can't say, "Quit your stressful job," "Yell at your bullyish boss," or even "Leave your somewhat annoying husband or wife." Instead, we have to deal with the stress that's given us. And that truly *is* like walking the tightrope.

OUTSIDE THE BOX

Kathy—Last year I went to the doctor for my yearly check-up. When he told me what I weighed, I blurted out, "Shut-up!" How could I be gaining weight when I was exercising four times a week? Unruffled by my near hysteria, the doctor said matter-of-factly, "It's muscle." I'm not Arnold Schwarzenegger, so how could I gain almost 15 pounds of muscle? To this my doctor chortled, "Hey, you're not a kid anymore." Once again I said, "Shut-up!" It took me a while to figure out that I was a stress eater. You would think that as a psychologist I would notice this, but I wasn't paying attention. My mind was someplace, but it sure wasn't in my head. There had been a lot of stress under my roof. My mother came to live with us and she was miserable. I was the unwitting target of her despair. My late-night splurges of peanuts and a glass of wine was packing on the pounds in spite of my exercising. My doctor was right, too. My body was changing, and my metabolism was slowing down. Even though I feel like I'm 25 years old, I'm not. I've made a few concessions. I still enjoy a glass of wine, but I keep the peanuts on the shelf where they belong.

Erica—If Kathy is a stress eater, I am a stress channel surfer. Not during primetime—I have *way* too much to do to watch TV during the hours from 8:00 p.m. to 11:30 p.m. But when it was time for bed and I wanted to unwind, I would just click, click, click my way through digital cable. That's 300 channels, folks. Finally, I realized this was an area I was "out of balance" about. I wasn't getting enough sleep, and though I was using it to reduce stress, it wasn't helping all that much. Now I try deep breathing, I got fantastic new pillows, and I treat my bedroom as a quiet zone. It helped (although I still consider Conan O'Brien and the late, late show a close companion).

De-Stressing

So if you can't quit your job or at least get a raise so you aren't stressing over bills, what can you do? And if you can't miraculously cure your teen of that attitude problem, what can you do? Because, as we said earlier, you would be dead without stress, you have two choices: (a) reduce the amount of stress or (b) change your *reaction* to stress.

Using our principle of small measurable steps, you can reduce stress by:

- ▲ Making conscious decisions to reduce stress by, for example, not watching the news or avoiding the talking heads on cable news that sometimes get your blood boiling.
- ▲ Sticking to a plan that gets you out of the house and away enjoying a relaxing hobby one night a week or part of a weekend day each week.
- ▲ Unplugging the phone and letting the machine pick up after 7:00 p.m.
- ▲ Not indulging your mother-in-law or stepbrother or father by reacting each time they press your proverbial buttons. Politely hang up and avoid the confrontation.
- ▲ If you work for a bully, at least polish your resume or take empowering steps in your career.

Chances are you already know some baby steps you can take to reduce stress in your life. The second choice is perhaps even more important. How do you react to stress? And how can you change that reaction if it's unhealthy.

You may think, "I've always blown my top . . . I'm hardwired that way." But you may be surprised to find that even heart attack victims and other people hardwired to react viscerally to stress have found ways to destress. These methods include:

- ▲ Biofeedback
- ▲ Meditation
- ▲ Yoga
- ▲ Prayer
- ▲ Journaling
- ▲ Therapy
- ▲ Exercise
- ▲ Support groups
- ▲ Healing power of laughter, pets, or other remedies

Taking baby steps, some of these methods need to be learned. Biofeedback, for instance, involves classes, usually at a hospital or therapeutic facility, in which actual body measurements, such as temperature or heart rate, are measured. Biofeedback has been used to conquer migraines (a common and sometimes stress-related illness), irritable bowel syndrome, and other illnesses.

However, exercise, prayer, or journaling can be something you can start trying today. Right now. You don't need fancy equipment—you just need a desire to change the way you react to stress.

The Good, the Bad, and the Ugly

In examining health and well-being, there are some things that aren't terrific for you, but in the grand scheme of things, they're okay. Carrying 10 extra pounds isn't the best thing in the world, but it's something you can likely conquer before it gets out of control. If you exercise two days a week, but you really need to increase that to four or five times, you at least have the start of a good plan.

There are, however, the bad and the ugly—those items that you really can't compromise on if you want balance and if you want to live a long and healthy life.

- ▲ *Smoking.* If you've never watched someone you love gasping for air because of emphysema or lung cancer, consider yourself blessed. The link to cancer is very clear-cut, and this is a habit you must break at all costs. There have been advances made with nicotine gum and patches and you will find that your doctor will most likely be thrilled if you want to quit. Or, you can try visiting www.smokenders.com.
- ▲ *Alcohol use.* In times of stress, this is often a flag that things are getting out of control. If you watch your drinking move from two cocktails a week on weekends to two strong cocktails a night to unwind, or if you are using alcohol to fall asleep (news flash: alcohol interferes with restful sleep), it is time to revisit your usage.
- ▲ *Recreational drugs or abuse of prescription medications.* Either of these can send you down a path to self-destruction.

- *Binge eating.* When you had your heart broken for the first time when you were 13, maybe you ate a pint of heavenly hash ice cream. Food is a pretty common comfort mechanism. Even the words "comfort food" bring to mind wonderful images for many people—anything from mashed potatoes or sweet potato pie to ice cream to Krispy Kreme donuts. But if the occasional indulgence is turning into secretive eating (hiding wrappers or stopping and eating before you come home for dinner) or eating until you feel sick, it's time to get help.
- *Not visiting the doctor or getting the recommended tests for your age.* A yearly physical with a physician you can confide in and trust is important. Also important are getting those tests appropriate for your age, whether that be a colonoscopy, cholesterol screening, blood pressure screening, mammogram, pap smear and so forth. Unfortunately, by the time most of us reach middle age, we will be aware of one or more tragic stories of someone who put off screening only to discover they had breast cancer or had colon cancer. We could fill this chapter with statistics on cancer, heart attacks, and silent killers like undiagnosed diabetes or high blood pressure, but it's simpler to say love yourself and your family enough to commit to regular check-ups and tests. Katie Couric, for instance, is a spokeswoman for colon cancer screening. Though a colonoscopy fills most people with feelings of embarrassment or dread, Couric had one done on national television! She showed that 10 to 20 minutes of being mildly uncomfortable is certainly worth your very life.

Balance Isn't Perfection

This book is about striking a balance. As such, balance is not perfection. In our introduction, we talked about childhood dreams. You wanted to be a right-fielder for the Yankees; you wanted to be an astronaut; you wanted to sing at the Metropolitan Opera. And maybe you've done that. But most likely you haven't. Many of us still hold those images in our mind along with other self-destructive ones.

For instance, many women succumb to Hollywood's beauty ideal. *Sure*, after you have a baby it would be nice if four weeks later you looked as svelte as Sarah Jessica Parker did after the birth of her child. Ladies! Face reality! Most of us could look that fantastic with a full-time trainer, air brushing, and a nanny who lets us get our beauty rest. Kudos to Parker for admitting as much when she was the cover girl of *W* magazine.

Think back to your high school physique. That shape is likely not possible in adulthood. What you *can* decide is to be in as best shape as you can be for your age and body type, and let go of unrealistic expectations of perfection.

It's time to write down your total health and wellness goals. You may be asking, why should I write them down? I want to be in great shape—period. Remember in the beginning of this chapter when we talked about fuzzy versus clear thinking? Saying that you want to be in great shape is another example of fuzzy thinking. You can't get an active plan in gear with your head full of murky thoughts. Knowing what you want in clear terms sets the stage for success. Writing goals down on paper makes them more real. Things look different on paper. You need to be able to recognize the signs or mile markers that you are moving in the right direction. As a reminder:

Fuzzy Thinking	**Clear Thinking**
I want to be in fantastic shape.→	I will make time to exercise five days a week by walking on my lunch hour and brown-bagging a healthy salad.

Write down your top five health and wellness goals:

1 ______________________________

2 ______________________________

3 ______________________________

4 ______________________________

5 ______________________________

Now, ask yourself this question:

On a scale ranging from 1 to 10, with 1 being "the worst," and 10 being "great," how well would you say you are taking care of your health and wellness right now?

If you answered with a 9 or 10, that's impressive. We salute you and say keep up the pace. Remember, though, that life has a way of throwing you a curve ball just when you think you have it all together. There are always unexpected health scares, the holidays when you fall off your dietary wagon, or times of high stress when you may have more than your customary glass of wine on the weekends. That doesn't demolish all your good work. You just need to "re-balance" again.

How have you managed to maintain your health and wellness so far? What is working for you?

What could you do to bring your score up half a notch, say to a 9 ½? If you gave yourself a 10, what can you continue to do to keep your score at a 10?

Many of us wouldn't give ourselves a high score when it comes to health. According to the CDC, we're an obese nation. We're a nation of size 14s looking at magazines with size zero models—who are *still* airbrushed to perfection.

In fact, many would score themselves lower than they actually should. What score did you give yourself? A two? Three? Five?

Ask yourself this question:

What kinds of things have you been doing to keep your score at a two or five? Think about it—you didn't give yourself a zero so you must be doing a few things correctly. What have you managed to do right?

If you are thinking that there simply couldn't be anything in a score that low, you're wrong. If you didn't give yourself a flat zero it is because in some small ways you are doing a few positive things to stay healthy. It may feel small or inconsequential but change is built on tiny, baby steps. A step in the right direction is powerful because it takes you closer to your goals. You may at least get your cholesterol checked. You may have banished the salt shaker at the kitchen table, even if you still have ice cream for dessert.

What is one more thing you can do to find balance in your health and wellness and bring your score up a point?

What will you do to ensure that you keep doing that one small thing?

How will your life be different when you manage to get your score up a few points?

____

____

What will you be doing that you are not doing now?

____

____

Who will be the most surprised about these healthful changes?

____

____

____

Falling Off the Wagon

A true sense of balance will come when you have made strides in your health and wellness goals—when you are changing the way you react to stress, when you are making time for important things like exercise, and when you have finally stomped out the smoking habit. Remember, life lived in balance is a matter of walking that tightrope. You may wobble from time to time. That's okay. Be gentle to yourself. Ease up on the self-criticism. Applaud the strides you are making, not only for yourself, but for those you love.

CHAPTER 5

YOUR CAREER IN THE BALANCE

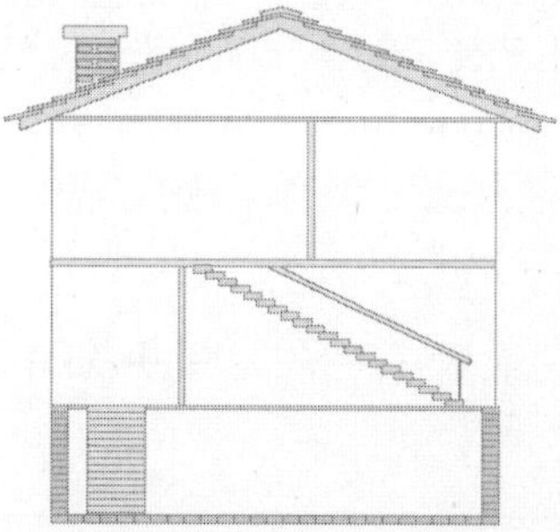

Everybody's chugging along in the same direction: Whether you are a recent college grad, baby boomer, 30-something, 40-something, computer geek, seasoned pro, first-timer, man, or woman. We all want to move ahead, enjoy our jobs, and live a satisfying lifestyle. It doesn't matter whether you own a kiosk in the mall, run a home office, or head a multimillion-dollar conglomerate.

Our work helps to define us and tells the world who we are. Are you where you want to be? When you look over your career or the type of work you do, is it what you had in mind? If your work fulfills you, our hats are off to you. We have a hunch that everyday a good number of people are out there going to jobs they dislike and feeling underpaid and overworked.

Do you think it's possible to use the words job and satisfying in the same sentence? We do. Is it easy? Probably not because if it was you would have already done it. Is it worth it? You're worth it. The important element is what you think you can or cannot do. We know from our own experiences that when a job is wrong or feels wrong you feel out of sorts, to say the least.

This chapter can assist you in teasing out how you view your job and career. You may be thinking, "I know how I view my job—it stinks," but that is not enough. Although you may feel that way and be justified in those feelings, saying you don't like your job doesn't get you anywhere. Examining why you feel that way and what you can do about it is a completely different story.

We encourage you to scribble in this book, make lists in it, and jot down all the ideas that pop into your head. Make this book your own. The questions in this chapter are intended for you to guide you to the place you want to be. Any change takes action. Ideas in your head are just like fish in a tank—swimming around, crashing into glass walls, and going nowhere.

What is the best part of your job? What aspects of your job do you value and consider assets?

1 ______________________________

2 ______________________________

3 ______________________________

4 ______________________________

5 ______________________________

Sometimes your work is not what you want it to be. Perhaps you feel underpaid, underappreciated, or trapped. You don't like the stress it brings. Professional achievement may sound like foreign words intended for somebody else. Consider the question that follows:

What aspects of your job would you like to change? What are the concerns that have been wearing you down?

1 ______________________________

2 ______________________________

3 ______________________________

4 ______________________________

5 ______________________________

What's your thinking style? Is it fuzzy or clear? If you're a fuzzy thinker you may sound like this, "I'm tired of this position." You make blanket statements that provide little information about what's really eating you. A clear thinker might say, "I have the experience to seek a management position in my company." The person who is a clear thinker is able to define what he or she wants.

If you want to make changes in your work life, then build a clear picture of what you're going for. You are walking through the fog unless you create a vivid image of what you need and where you wish to go.

Instead of Fuzzy Thinking	Think Clearly
I want to move ahead. →	I have the experience to pursue an administrative position.
I feel stifled by my position. →	I want a position that enables me to use my marketing background and has opportunities for advancement.
The stress of this job is wearing me out. →	I want a position with flexible hours and the ability to work from my home office.

Looking for Pearls?

When it comes to hunting for jobs and professional opportunities, one of the most effective strategies anyone can do is to network. Whoever first said, "It's not what you know, but who you know," knew exactly what he or she was talking about. Where should you network, when, and with whom? That's easy to answer—everywhere, all the time, and with everyone. We are surrounded by opportunities to network:

- ▲ Community organizations
- ▲ Clubs
- ▲ Conferences

- ▲ Professional associations
- ▲ Colleagues and coworkers
- ▲ Cocktail parties
- ▲ Family gatherings
- ▲ Hair salon
- ▲ Golf course
- ▲ Place of worship
- ▲ Weddings, baby showers, and block parties
- ▲ Sports club

Are you getting the idea? Remember—the world is small. You never know who you are going to meet. Sometimes the most unlikely individual has a wealth of contacts, "You wrote a book about fighter pilots? My brother's an executive producer for the History Channel. I'm sure he'll want to interview you."

Here are a few tips for the next time you find yourself in a room full of opportunities:

1. *First, learn to speak in sound bites.* Turn on your television and watch how public figures and news people answer questions. Better still, time their answer. Public figures speak in 10-, 20-, and 30-second sound bites. Like a boxer trying to land an upper cut, they get in and out fast. They are savvy to the fact that they only have a short amount of time to make their point and keep your attention. This same rule should apply to you when you are networking.
2. *Be prepared to answer these questions—What kind of work would you like to do?* Your answer ought to be clear and concise. The person you're speaking with should walk away with a clear idea of what you want to do. Vague answers become fuzzy and quickly forgotten.

Avoid Fuzzy Statements	Make Clear Statements
I want to work in communications. →	I want to be a radio sports announcer.
I want to work in the fashion industry. →	I want to be a makeup artist for a leading women's magazine.
I'm interested in working in graphic design. →	I'm looking to design book covers and promotional materials for a graphic design company.

3. *What are your qualifications?* Be able to describe your qualifications and experience quickly. In fact, under a minute or less is best. This isn't the time to blather on about your scientific research into drosophila cross-breeding. You may think it's fascinating, but the person you're speaking with is likely to glaze over and slip into a trance. Instead, briefly state where you went to school, trained, and any experience you might have had.
4. *Can you leave them with a dazzler?* A dazzler is some exceptional skill or experience that is sure to get that person's attention and make them remember you. This is your opportunity to leave the person with lasting image of who you are.
5. *Keep a business card handy.* Get into the habit of carrying business cards because people will ask you for them. Phone numbers scribbled on cocktail napkins undoubtedly get lost and forgotten. If you don't work for a company, then make your own. There are great Internet sites where you can design your own card and have it shipped to you in a few days. Www.vistaprint.com is a terrific site not only for business cards, but also for promotional cards and stationary.
6. *Be willing to reciprocate.* Be alert for opportunities to help other people. Sometimes you can meet someone who would be a great contact for your friend or business associate. If you do pass on someone's name, give them a call to let them know you have done so. This way they can follow up with a phone call or a visit. Even if the opportunity or contact doesn't work out, he or she will remember that you tried.

OUTSIDE THE BOX

Kathy—Back in 1994 I had a full-time private practice in Boca Raton. The office was beautiful, but I was miserable. More to the point, I was bored out of my mind. All day long I sat in one chair and listened to other people. Most of the time the insurance companies paid poorly or not at all. The sudden arrival of my son from Vietnam was all the inspiration I needed to change my career path. I went into publishing. So many people shook their heads disapprovingly and asked, "How could you throw away your Ph.D. like that? All that schooling for nothing." I didn't see it that way at all. I was taking that Ph.D. and my experience and following my passion. I have never looked back.

Erica—Anyone who knows me instantly recognizes that me and a 9-to-5 job are like oil and water. Been there, done that. Done well. But I was always the woman who was putting on her makeup in the car on the way to work. I struggled to be on time. I hated being a slave to the clock . . . and meetings? Save me from another long-winded one, please. When I started my own editorial company, part of me felt like I was walking off the plank of a pirate ship, but I knew if I didn't, I'd always wonder "should I have?" "could I have?" Eight years later, the thought of a desk job still makes me scream for the hills, but I have been able to have much more balance—and income—by being an entrepreneur. The jump off the plank was successful for me.

Write Your Own Map

Stop here for a moment and consider exactly where you would like to go in your professional life. Maybe your dreams aren't huge—you just want your coworkers to stop interrupting you a hundred times a day or you feel ready to take on more responsibility in your department. Maybe you *do* dream big. Your dream is to be the largest distributor of Australian wine in the United States. It doesn't matter; you still need a plan to succeed.

What are your professional goals? (Remember to be specific and measurable.) What concerns would you like to resolve?

1 ______________________________

2 ______________________________

3 ______________________________

4 ______________________________

5 ______________________________

Don't skip ahead because this next part is important. There really is something to that creative visualization talk. Most successful people will tell you that they had a visual image of where they were going. Imagine for a moment that you have accomplished everything on your career list. Answer this question:

What will your life be like when you have reached your career goals? What will your life be like when these professional concerns are behind you? What will you be doing?

1 ______________________________

2 ______________________________

3 ______________________________

4 ______________________________

5 ______________________________

Finally, think about this next question. If you're creating a map to get you to your goals, then you will need to know the first mile-marker you will see as you succeed in changing your professional life.

What will be the smallest signs that you are moving in the right direction and away from your job stressors? Remember—think small.

1 ______________________________

2 ______________________________

3 ______________________________

4 ______________________________

5 ______________________________

Small does not mean insignificant, but rather, it increases the likelihood that you will achieve your goals. Bigger signs will appear, but not before that tiny clue that indicates things are starting to happen.

Too Big	Just Right
I'll land that Webster Technology account. →	I will set up a meeting with the financial controller for Webster Technology.
I'll open a ladies-only workout center. →	I'll research available franchises and do a study of workout centers in my community.
I want a raise. →	I'll look into what others are being paid in my position before I approach my boss.

As you can see, it's a wise idea to start with small signs. It is a step in the direction you want to go. It is your plan. We may live in a fast-paced society, but career changes frequently take more time. Often our career doesn't move along as fast as our dreams. If you plunge ahead with just your ambition and without your head, your goals will take longer to reach. Consider this advice as you consider the changes you want to make in your career.

- ▲ *Keep in mind that everything looks greener in* their *backyard.* It's only human nature to think that successful people got to where they are by crossing theirs arms, blinking twice, and wiggling their nose. The reality is that nearly every one of them paid their dues with long hours and hard work.
- ▲ *When you get the ball, run.* Often the one defining moment in a successful person's life is that when they were given the opportunity to get ahead, they took it.

What work issues keep repeating over and over in your job?

1 ____

2 ____

3 ____________________

4 ____________________

5 ____________________

What is your typical way of handling these concerns?

1 ____________________

2 ____________________

3 ____________________

4 ____________________

5 ____________________

How would your family and friends say you usually handle these concerns?

1 ____________________

2 ____________________

3 ____________________

4 ____________________

5 ____________________

Take some time and think about your job and career goals. Once again, keep in mind that to get where you want to go, you first need to know where you are going.

Write down your top five goals toward having a more satisfying career:

1 ____________________

2 ____________________

3 ____________________

4 ____________________

5 ____________________

Now ask yourself this question:

On a scale ranging from 1 to 10, with 1 being "the worst," and 10 being "great," how well would you say you are taking care of your career right now?

How have you managed to keep a strong career so far? What is working for you?

What could you do to bring your score up half a notch, say to 9 ½? If you gave yourself a 10, what can you continue to do to keep your score at a 10?

If you notice that your scores are on the low end, then ask yourself this question:

What kinds of things have you been doing to keep your score at a two or five? Think about it —you didn't give yourself a zero so you must be doing a few things correctly. What have you managed to do right?

If you're coming to the conclusion that with scores this low you'll end up without a friend in the world, you're wrong. If you didn't write down a zero, maybe it's because you have realized that there are a few redeeming signs about your job.

What's that, you say? You can't find anything positive to say about the old 9-to-5? Then think smaller.

What is one more small thing you can do in your career to bring your score up a point?

____

____

____

What will you do to ensure that you keep doing that one small thing?

____

____

____

How will your life be different when you manage to get your score up a few points?

____

____

____

What will you be doing that you are not doing now?

____

____

____

Who will be the most surprised about these positive changes?

____

____

____

Balancing Work, Family, and You

Balancing your job, family, and you is more than a tightrope walk. Some days it's more like an audition for Cirque de Soleil. You balance your steps, wobble a bit, and hold on tight by your toes. To close this chapter, we leave you with a few tips for staying up on your wire:

- Establish and keep a workable routine in your household so that everyone knows what to expect.
- Get up before the kids and take care of your needs first.
- Have your day organized the night before.
- Keep in contact with your children's teachers via email.
- Take notice of the things that stress you out and eliminate whatever you can (kids and spouse not included).
- You don't have to say yes to everything; in fact, practice saying the word no in the mirror. Make the commitments that matter most.
- Find the time to play and just relax. You not only deserve it, you need it.
- Divvy up the household chores with everyone. Even little ones can help out in some way.
- Build an exercise routine into your life.
- Hire a babysitter and go out as a couple at least once a month.
- Stop procrastinating and start doing what needs to get done. Even a little bit at a time is better than having anxiety over a growing "to-do" list.
- As cliché as it sounds—don't sweat the small stuff.
- Focus on all that's positive in your life.

CHAPTER 6

BALANCE AND EMOTIONAL BAGGAGE: WHAT'S KEEPING YOU DOWN?

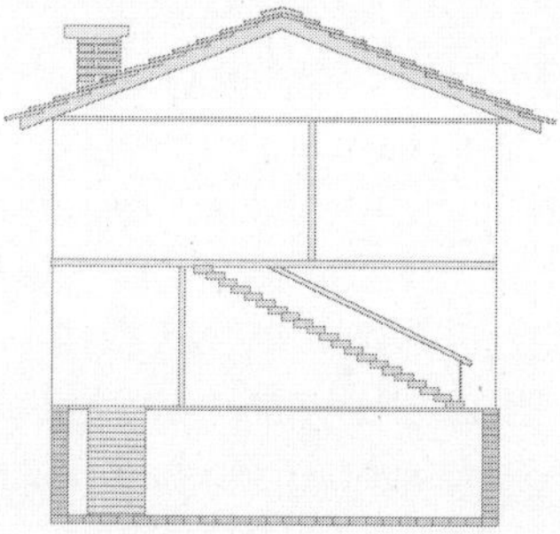

We all have it. We go through life lugging behind us a giant trunk full of emotional baggage. For some of us, the load is light. For others, the trunk might as well be a moving van—the really big one. Some of the things we lug around with us are from childhood. Other baggage can be from the more recent past. Though you often hear psychologists talk about "family of origin," "dysfunctional families," and the like, not all our baggage wounds have to do with Mom and Dad. In fact, wounds from our careers can hurt almost as much: the bullying boss, the back-stabbing coworker, the unceremonious firing. When taking stock of your emotional baggage consider some of these scenarios:

- ▲ One or both of your parents had a drinking problem or, a caustic tongue, or nothing you ever did felt "good enough." Your father flew off the handle at a moment's notice. Your mother was only concerned about the country club.
- ▲ You have adult siblings who impinge on you emotionally. Maybe you have a brother who's a freeloader or a sister who's on her fifth divorce and you're always the one they call in to pick up the pieces.

- ▲ You have old wounds from your present or former employer. We have all known people who have been unjustly fired, had their hard work unrecognized, or had someone take credit for their brilliant ideas.
- ▲ You have wounds from your marriage or your ex-marriage that you still haven't dealt with yet. You find it hard to be around your spouse or ex-spouse without bitter-sounding comments springing from your mouth, almost without you thinking about it.

Whatever the baggage you carry around with you, the consequences are another burden of stress that can certainly throw you out of balance. If the wounds are deep enough, it can lead to sickness. Irritable bowel syndrome, for instance, is often considered stress-related.

A friend of ours recently said, "When did I turn into a shrew?" She was shocked to really "hear" how she was speaking to her husband—whom she had not fully forgiven for an affair of 10 years ago. Believe us, affairs are probably the hardest thing to get over—and many, many marriages don't survive them. It wasn't so much that she was still angry that shocked her, but when she *heard* herself, she could actually hear the pain still there coming out as hostility. This type of nagging or bickering—over anything from an affair to wounds about division of household labor—can be the result of not dealing with your baggage. Suddenly your baggage is dragging you around by the collar, not the other way around. It's like having a pet lion that you keep fairly docile, even have it jump through hoops like in the circus . . . and suddenly the lion is uncontrollable. Now you're jumping through hoops and the lion is in charge.

Bullying at Work

A United Kingdom "Bad Boss" hotline cited 38% of callers had a bullying boss (www.bullyonline.org).

Whatever issues you are carrying around with you, if you do not at some point delve into those "dark places" in yourself and bring the problems out into the light, they will continue to gnaw at you. Emotional baggage can weigh you down and make you chronically tired or depressed. Isn't it time to lighten your load?

Before we delve into letting go of your unwanted burdens, we must stop and say that if you have suicidal thoughts, issues of extreme gravity like sexual abuse or alcoholism, or severe depression going on for longer than two weeks, it is probably time to seek professional help. If you need more information about the signs and symptoms of depression, try www.learn-about-depression.com. If you have thoughts about hurting yourself, call 1-800-NEW HOPE. Whatever you do, seek help.

Now, turning to things you may want to tackle yourself, using the same thinking we'll apply throughout the book, it isn't enough to say, "I want to be rid of my emotional baggage." Broad statements, what we have been calling fuzzy thinking, are almost akin to "wishful thinking." You can't just "decide" to do away with those resentments, pains, and hurts you may have been lugging around for most of your life. You can, in the interest of finding some balance in your life, make some specific goals when it comes to ridding yourself of past hurts.

Instead of Fuzzy Thinking	Think clearly
I don't want to be angry at my alcoholic parents anymore. →	I will try Adult Children of Alcoholics meetings, attending four meetings to decide if this organization may help me or not.
I want to let go of my old feelings about my ex-boss who fired me. →	I will try short-term therapy to "talk out" some of my anger. I will write down all my feelings about this person and then burn the letter to let go of some of my resentment. I will exercise four days a week, because I know that will help me burn off some of this stress.

The idea with fuzzy versus clear thinking, again, is to take some measurable action. It isn't enough to "want" to be rid of something. It also isn't helpful to have broad goals and agendas. You want something manageable so that you can see for yourself that you are making progress.

Write Your Own Map

Like the woman we mentioned who said she was shocked that she had become a "shrew," or the man we know who still can't eat dinner with his father without it turning into a shouting match, none of us sets out in life to drag old bitterness with us. And there are few feelings worse than waking each morning for work with a knot in your stomach or facing the holidays with dread. Now it's time to take those resentments out into the light of day so you can see what you would specifically like to resolve.

What are your goals as far as shedding your emotional baggage? (Remember to be specific and measurable.) What problems would you like to resolve?

1 ______________________________

2 ______________________________

3 ______________________________

4 ______________________________

5 ______________________________

This next part is important. Imagine for a moment that you have accomplished everything on your wellness list. Answer this question:

What will your life be like when these resentments no longer have any weight? What will you be doing? Imagine the freedom. Imagine waking without that "rock" feeling in the pit of your stomach.

____

____

____

____

____

____

Now, as you ponder this, please also shut off any old "tapes" that are going to be negative. Maybe you feel like you can *never* forgive your best friend at work for stealing your ideas—and that promotion that should have been yours. But don't use absolutes like never. Say "for today I cannot let go, but perhaps tomorrow I can."

Finally, think for another moment and answer this question. This question is important because it's the first mile-marker you're going to see as you take yourself to a better emotional life.

What will be the smallest sign that you are moving in the right direction and that you are moving away from old resentments? You want to list this sign so that you can see your progress and recognize it.

____

____

When there is a positive change in one area, other positive changes will occur somewhere else. If you think of life as walking that tightrope, the balancing act is an art form unto itself. But like a true tightrope walker, you cannot afford to feel wobbly and pulled in different directions. You will feel stressed and unbalanced. The positive effects of letting go of old baggage may reverberate through your health and wellness (less stress-related illness) or through your job (your new, positive attitude may win you new fans in the executive office). So think small goals, no matter how unimportant it may seem, and how far you may feel from your larger goals, and know even baby steps can help you restore balance into your life.

Too Big	**Just Right**
I will forgive my parents and spend blissful Christmas holidays with them.→	This week when my mother calls, I will count to 10 before answering her when she asks me why I haven't gotten that new promotion.
I will forgive my ex-wife and we will start attending all school functions together. →	I will resolve not to make any snide comments about my ex-wife in front of the children this week.

Too Big	Just Right
I will forgive my bullying boss for humiliating me in front of the department for the millionth time this week. →	I will polish my resume as a sign I may really be ready to leave this place.

It really is a good idea to start with small signs. Avoid all or nothing thinking, and avoid being too ambitious. For instance, we know a woman who suffered through an abusive childhood and then went into an abusive marriage and—you guessed it—had a bullying boss. She attended a seminar about "forgiveness," but the abuse she suffered was so terrible immediate and absolute forgiveness would really have been a tall order. This set her up for failure and then more self-criticism ("Why can't I forgive? I'm not doing it 'right.'") A better solution would have been to take small steps toward letting go of her old pain—such as finding a support group; writing unmailed letters to her abusers so she could vent her feelings; finding a therapist; and resolving to make one new, positive role model friend.

Why Now Is Better than Later

In the quest for balance, there is no time like the present. Many of us avoid looking at our "old issues." We feel we should be "past that." Or we may truly have lived through something horrific—a divorce by a vengeful spouse that bankrupted us or harmed our relationship with our children or an abusive family member who remains a bitter, cruel person—and it hurts to delve backwards. We may feel we should be over things by now. Or, quite frankly, the veritable glut of self-help books has turned people off from finding help. There are comedians who make light of the "dysfunctional family"—after all, aren't we *all* dysfunctional in some way or another? But our guess is a still, small voice inside tells you that sooner or later you have to deal with your past resentments. There are clues—stress-related illnesses that come up again and again (such as the "flu"

Stress in America

The American Institute of Stress, located in New York, was founded in 1978 and is a clearinghouse of information about stress, including what they say is one of the top culprits: job stress.

you get every Thanksgiving, the instant tension in your neck every time you see your boss, the sweaty palms every time Caller ID says your father is calling). These old baggage issues aren't going to vaporize and disappear without work. You'll just bury them deeper and deeper. So the question we ask you is this one: Wouldn't you rather deal with this now and get it over with and move along in your quest for balance, rather than dealing with these *same* issues 10 years from now (with 10 more years of these rotten feelings and stress reactions)?

Headaches, stomachaches, shoulder tension, irritability—what are the signs and symptoms that old issues are keeping you from your full potential today?

1 ______________________________

2 ______________________________

3 ______________________________

4 ______________________________

5 ______________________________

Now is the time to rid yourself of the aches, pains, and unhappiness that emotional baggage brings with it.

OUTSIDE THE BOX

KATHY: For years I tried to nurture a friendship with my first husband. Every now and then I would give him a call or drop a note just to check in. I genuinely cared and wished him well. We were both happily remarried. I even felt good that in spite of a divorce we could somehow forge a friendship. How many people could actually make that claim? Last fall, good friends told me that my ex-husband speaks terribly about me to anyone with a set of ears. In fact, his critical comments nearly severed a ghostwriting job with a celebrity. For a few months I was wounded, but then I realized a few things. Our friendship was the result of my efforts and not his. I was his friend, but he wasn't mine. People don't change just because you do. Sometimes people remain who they are. I let that relationship go and I feel freer. Now the friendships I choose are with people who have a genuine interest in being friends with me.

ERICA: My family is a blended one, albeit one that has been blended since my oldest child was two. For some time after divorcing my first husband, my ex-in-laws and I needed room to figure out our relationship, especially in light of the fact that my ex-husband and I do not get along to this day. I am proud to say that for my daughter's sake, I have even vacationed with her paternal grandparents and my current husband. Her grandmother passed away this summer, and I have no regrets over the friendship I forged with her. She was my ex-mother-in-law, but I considered her a friend, and it was good to leave old baggage having to do with her son in the dust and simply move on for my child's sake. I think we both taught my daughter something valuable along the way about grace and dignity.

You Can't Run and You Can't Hide

We all have the fantasy. Running away from it all for a while. Come on . . . haven't you ever pictured being swept away to a deserted island; taking a permanent vacation at Club Med; ditching house, spouse, and kids and disappearing to a tranquil cabin in the woods somewhere? Whatever your fantasy, it all revolves around one word: escape.

Unfortunately, even if you take some baby steps toward unloading old "stuff," it's a constantly evolving process. You may feel like you have forgiven Monster Boss today, but three weeks from now you may find that the resentment has landed right in the pit of your stomach again. That's okay. But constantly evolving or not, you can't run from heavy baggage. It will find you—even in the middle of the night, waking you up and causing insomnia or restless sleep.

Another problem is very often we have baggage related to people we can't just excise out of our lives—like ex-spouses we have to interact with because of our children, parents, siblings, coworkers, even our own kids.

Using our principle of small measurable steps, you can reduce your baggage in baby steps by:

- Making conscious decisions to reduce stress related to this person. For instance, visit Mom and Dad in Peoria for that four-day weekend, but opt to stay in a hotel so you have your own space and a place to decompress every night.
- Learning some positive stress-busters like meditation, deep breathing, journaling, and yoga.
- Seeking support groups if you have issues related to family alcoholism or abuse.
- Not indulging your mother-in-law or stepbrother or father by reacting each time they press your proverbial buttons. If you are feeling particularly vulnerable, screen your calls until you are in a better place to handle the usual conflicts.
- If you work for a bully, at least polish your resume or take empowering steps in your career.

Chances are you already know some baby steps you can take to reduce emotional baggage in your life.

The F-Word: Forgiveness

Probably the most controversial aspect of letting go of emotional baggage is the issue of forgiveness. Pick up any one of a hundred self-help books out there, and they will say forgiveness is essential for moving on and you must do it for you. This is often sound advice, but we also know people who have survived "the unforgivable." What is the unforgivable? Rape, murder, incest, vicious acts of betrayal . . . the heavy hitters of emotional baggage. We know people so badly abused they still sleep with the lights on. So must they forgive these heinous sins?

Frankly, we think not. We advocate (a) looking at the pain, not hiding from it and (b) moving on, but not necessarily forgiving. We can all parrot the "forgiveness" is the "right" thing to do party line. But why? If someone murdered one of our loved ones, we would have to find a way to deal with that. (See Chapter 11 for more on this topic.) Whether it is a philosophy of "bad things happen to good people" or a philosophy of existentialism, we all need to make sense of the most senseless of acts. September 11, for instance, calls upon every person touched by that tragedy to make some sort of peace with what they lost. Forgiveness may be a part of that. But if you can't get to the "F word," settle instead for finding a way to have peace by processing the pain until it's no longer so visceral.

Ready to Move On?

Now it's time to balance your world with clear ideas of your goals in the emotional baggage arena.

Write down your top five goals toward letting go of old pain.

1 ____

2 ____

3 ____

4 ____

5 ____

Now ask yourself this question:

On a scale ranging from 1 to 10, with 1 being "the worst," and 10 being "great," how well would you say you are taking care of your old resentments right now?

____

____

If you answered with a 9 or 10, that's impressive. But stick around because there is always more to learn. Remember that life has a way of throwing you a curve ball just when you think you have it all together. Remember how we said you may have felt like you moved on regarding your best friend who stole your spouse or harmed you, only to find those bad feelings landing in your stomach again three weeks from now?

> *How have you managed to maintain your sense of balance in this area so far?* What is working for you? *(Give yourself some well-deserved credit!)*

____

____

____

> *What could you do to bring your score up half a notch, say to a 9½? If you gave yourself a 10, what can you continue to do to keep your score at a 10?*

____

____

____

____

If you are full of old resentments and gave yourself a low score, ask yourself this question:

> *What kinds of things have you been doing to keep your score at a two or five? Think about it—you didn't give yourself a zero so you must be doing a few things correctly. What have you managed to do right?*

____

____

____

____

If you are thinking that there simply couldn't be anything in a score that low, you're wrong. If you didn't give yourself a flat zero it is because in some small ways you are doing a few positive things to be emotionally healthy. It may feel small or inconsequential but change is built on tiny, baby steps. A step in the right direction is powerful because it takes you closer to your goals. You didn't take the bait when your ex called. You spoke civilly to your nemesis at the company picnic.

What is one more thing you can do to find balance in your emotional life and bring your score up a point?

____

____

____

What will do you do to ensure that you keep doing that one small thing?

____

____

How will your life be different when you manage to get your score up a few points?

____

____

What will you be doing that you are not doing now?

____

____

Who will be the most surprised about these positive changes?

____

____

____

The Tightrope Wobbles

A true sense of balance will come when you wake up one morning keenly aware that you don't have a headache as you head off to work. Or your ex-spouse will call you because he or she messed up the visitation schedule *yet again*, and you just shrug and say, "Okay, what can we do to fix it?"

But if you wobble on that tightrope, know that life is full of the winds of change. It's okay if the headache returns tomorrow. It's all about making progress and changing your life to a more balanced picture one step at a time.

CHAPTER 7

MARRIAGE: THE TEST OF TIME

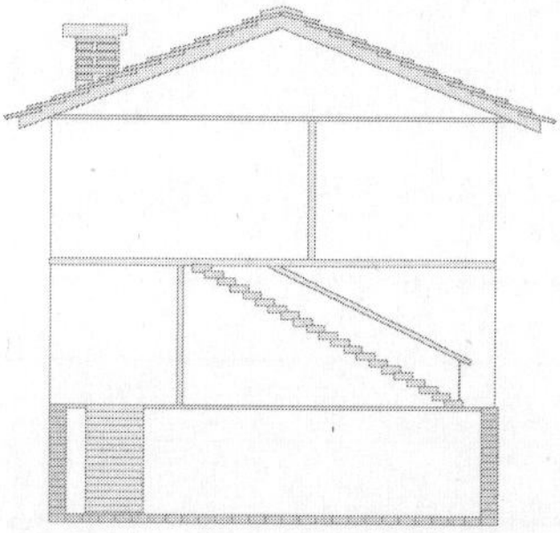

A wise old relationship expert once commented that the secret to a happy marriage wasn't endurance but good management. When two people commit to spend their lives together they are entering into years of decision making, negotiating, and problem solving.

Marriage Is Good for Your Health

Compared with unmarried people, married men and women tend to have lower mortality, less risky behavior, more monitoring of health, more compliance with medical regimens, higher sexual frequency, more satisfaction with their sexual lives, more financial savings, and higher wages (CDC, Advance Data, May 31, 2001).

This chapter is for everyone, whether you are in a satisfying marriage, a turbulent marriage, living with somebody, or dating. We all come with baggage—old relationships, a few skeletons, insecurities, and last but not least, our families. Sometimes you're lucky and the relationship moves along swimmingly. At other times it can feel as if there is one problem after another.

From time to time, we all have issues about our relationships. Often it only takes one problem to upset the stability of your marriage. Before you decide that nothing is going right in your marriage, you need to make some observations. What do you like about your relationship with your partner? What would you like to see change? When was the last time you considered the positive qualities of your marriage—or can't you remember? Throughout this book we encourage you to get your thoughts, ideas, feelings, and concerns out of your head and onto paper where you can see them. Everything looks different in black and white. If you're lucky, you will notice that there is more going well in your marriage than things that are wrong. Keep in mind that it only takes one sour feeling to ruin the taste of your relationship.

What is the best part of your marriage? What aspects of your marriage do you value and consider assets?

1. ______________________________
2. ______________________________
3. ______________________________
4. ______________________________
5. ______________________________

On the backside, what aspects of your marriage would you like to change? What are the concerns that have been wearing you down?

1. ______________________________
2. ______________________________
3. ______________________________
4. ______________________________
5. ______________________________

In this chapter and throughout this book we make reference to fuzzy versus clear thinking. We do that because it's our belief that the best way to get nowhere fast is to not know where you're going. If your thinking is fuzzy, you'll end up chasing your own tail. It's not enough to say that you want a better marriage. You need to know where to begin. What's more, you need to be able to recognize small signs that the relationship is changing for the better.

Instead of Fuzzy Thinking	Think Clearly
I want us to do more things together. →	We will hire a babysitter for Saturday nights.
We need a better sex life. →	I will initiate sex once a week.
We need to communicate better. →	I will ask my wife how her day went and share something about my day with her.
I want us to stop our chronic bickering. →	The next time we start to bicker I will count to 10 and not make a sarcastic comment.

Mirages of Marriage

Myths about marriage are so imbedded into our belief system that it can be difficult to know what's true from what's not. Myths have a tendency to play with our insecurities and ring our emotional bells. Nowhere is that more true than the subject of marriage. We want to be happily married, but can we? When it comes to marriage, who doesn't want to live out the fantasy in which our every wish and desire is met? Regardless of your relationship choices, it's tough to avoid the bombardment of myths.

- *Myth:* Everybody is supposed to get married.

  Reality: Sure, that sounds like a great plan. It's right up there with everyone is supposed to have children.

- *Myth:* Marriage will straighten your partner out.

  Reality: How many people have stepped into this booby trap? If you have concerns about your partner prior to marriage, chances are those same concerns will still be there once you're married. Ask yourself, "Do I want to get married to this person or do I just want to get married?"

- *Myth:* Children will make your marriage closer.

  Reality: Whoever started this rumor was obviously single and has never had a six-year-old vomiting in his or her bed at three in the morning. The truth is that a marriage ought to be strong prior to the arrival of children.

- *Myth:* The only difference between marriage and living together is a "piece of paper."

  Reality: That's not what the research shows. In fact, research shows that not only do married couples live longer than unmarried couples, but they are also healthier, more fulfilled, and have more money in the bank.

- *Myth:* In a good marriage, couples never go to bed angry.

  Reality: This one's a classic, straight out of an *I Love Lucy* episode. *As if* you could robotically control your feelings at the stroke of midnight with the expectation of getting a good night's rest.

- *Myth:* In a strong marriage, couples never fight (especially in front of the c-h-i-l-d-r-e-n).

  Reality: When a couple says that they never argue, you have to wonder if they're living under the same roof. When it comes to children, worry less about the fact that you argue and more about how you argue. Keep in mind that your children are watching how you resolve disagreements. If they never see you resolve a disagreement, how will they learn?

- *Myth:* Single people have better sex lives than married people.

  Reality: You may be surprised to hear that married couples report greater satisfaction in their sex lives than single folks.

- *Myth:* In a great marriage, couples do everything together.

  Reality: Be serious. You're both individuals, not twins connected at the hip. There is nothing wrong with couples having separate interests and activities. Pursuing your own interests can invigorate a marriage.

- *Myth:* A great marriage means that you ought to vent all your feelings toward your spouse.

  Reality: Just because you are married doesn't mean that you can blurt out stinging barbs and your partner is supposed to accept it. Some verbal attacks can't be taken back. More than a few marriages have been damaged because someone can't get past a severe tongue-lashing.

▲ *Myth:* Marriage means that you will never be lonely again.

Reality: There are many lonely people both in and out of marriage. You are responsible for making yourself happy, not your partner.

Myths are exactly that—myths. You and your partner are what's real. Stop peeking over the fence to see what other couples are doing. It's a well-worn saying, but "the grass always looks greener on the other side."

OUTSIDE THE BOX

Kathy—I have very vivid memories of how my parents would argue when I was a little girl. My father was quiet and easygoing. My mother was like a tsunami rolling into the shore. She would throw vases, ashtrays, or anything else she could grab. I remember one night at the dinner table watching a steak knife sailing into the wall above our heads. My brothers and I kept our eyes down on our plates while my father ignored the whole thing. I wasn't so much scared as I was puzzled by it. Today I am fortunate to be married to a great guy. We can get mad at each other from time to time, but we talk it out. I realize now that he is a lot like my father. At 85, my mom is a little less feisty, but she'd still throw an ashtray at your head if she could get at it.

Erica—In seeking *balance,* I have come to understand that life is about picking your battles. My husband once asked me, "So what are you gonna do? Go to divorce court and tell the judge you want to be granted a divorce because I leave my socks on the floor and won't pick up the newspaper?" Actually, I do think that is legitimate grounds for divorce in certain states. But I have learned to pay to have a housekeeper come once a week rather than seethe over the "little things" that drive me crazy. It's better for the blood pressure. The little stuff can get to you, but don't forget the big picture. And if my husband is reading this . . . clean up once in a while, will you?

g Fair

ople cannot spend years together raising children, maintaining a home, holding jobs, paying down debt, and dealing with in-laws and not disagree from time to time. When it comes to fighting, we're all a little different. Some of us bicker and verbally spar with each other constantly. Others can go for months, maybe longer, without so much as a misunderstanding. The bottom line is not that you argue, but how you argue. Do your disputes morph into volcanic eruptions and character assassinations? Everybody's entitled to speak their mind and get things off their chest. But a marriage license is not a license to act like a prima dona or an immature bully. Here's some advice for when the going gets tough:

- *Hold your tongue (even if it kills you).* Sometimes a situation can arise that makes you so mad that you swear your head is going to blow up. Getting a concern off your chest is one thing, but flinging insults and derogatory comments is both childish and hurtful.
- *Keep your fighting private.* If you are angry about something then wait until you can be alone with your partner to discuss it. It's not fair to make family and friends uncomfortable because of something that doesn't involve them.
- *Stick to the subject.* Don't switch subjects or throw in old business just because you're ticked off.
- *Act civilized.* Just because you're in the heat of an argument doesn't mean that you should lose all sense of civility toward one another. It's an argument, not the *Battle of Midway*. Stop being so concerned that you be right that you can't get your partner something to drink or a chair to sit in. Second, let the other person speak.
- *Pick your battles.* Is it really necessary to go 12 rounds over everything? Is finding there's no toilet paper really worth having a fight over? Decide what you can ignore and what you feel is important. If you're going off over every blessed thing, sooner or later your partner is going to tune you out.
- *If you feel yourself losing control, leave the room.* There may be moments in an intense argument when you feel like throwing some-

thing or even striking your partner. In those instances, be wise and leave the room until you get your anger under control. If you feel this is something hard to control you may want to consider getting some outside help.

▲ *When it's over, it's over.* Once you've resolved a disagreement then put it behind you. Bite your lip when you feel the urge to dish it up again.

Write Your Own Map

Time and time again, we have come across people who believe that they cannot change the course of their lives. Like a script handed down at birth, these friends and colleagues view their lives as something to endure or get through. They cannot imagine that they have the power to effect change in their life. How sad is that?

Ask someone what he or she would like to see different in their marriage. The answer is usually negative, for instance, "I don't want to keep fighting over the same things all the time" or "I want my wife to stop driving me nuts." The problem is that these statements are really complaints and don't describe where you want to go or what you need to change. The trouble with focusing on complaints is that you're not thinking about what can be done about them.

Instead of Saying	Say
I want my wife to get off my back. →	I'd like to be able to talk with my wife.
I hate the way my husband just lies around the house all weekend. →	I'd like my husband and I to make weekend plans.
I am disgusted with the way we handle our finances.→	I want to create a schedule for paying and filing our bills.

This is a good time to think about what you want for marriage. Even though it is tempting to write down all the things that bug you about your partner—resist. Instead, write down what you would like to see happen in your marriage that is not happening right now.

What are your goals for your marriage? (Remember to be specific and measurable.) What concerns would you like to resolve?

1. ______________________________
2. ______________________________
3. ______________________________
4. ______________________________
5. ______________________________

Don't skip over this next part. Imagine for a moment that you have accomplished everything on your marriage list. Now answer this question:

What will your life be like when these concerns no longer have an effect on your relationship? What will you be doing? What will you be enjoying that you are not enjoying at this moment?

1. ______________________________
2. ______________________________
3. ______________________________
4. ______________________________
5. ______________________________

Last, but not least, think for a few more seconds and consider this question. It is important because it's the first road sign you will come to as you strengthen and improve your marriage.

What will be the smallest signs that you are moving in the right direction and away from those aspects of your marriage that have frustrated or disappointed you? Remember—think small.

1. ______________________________
2. ______________________________
3. ______________________________
4. ______________________________
5. ______________________________

We cannot emphasize enough the importance of thinking small when it comes to making changes in your relationship. Any change can be difficult, but your plans will likely fail if you take on too much at once. Be patient. One small positive step is still a step—and in the right direction.

Too Big	Just Right
I want to put romance back into my marriage. →	I am going to talk with my wife about ways to spend more time together.
I'm going to stop fighting with my husband. →	I am going to count to 10 whenever I feel myself getting angry.
I am going to stop undermining my wife's authority with the children. →	I will speak with my wife privately the next time I disagree with the way she disciplines the children.

How to Drive Your Partner Nuts

A marriage isn't just about one person. It's a partnership that with love and good management will endure for a lifetime. Nobody comes into a relationship without flaws and quirks. Sometimes we're not even aware of the ways we can drive our partner crazy. Read on to see if you see yourself:

- ▲ *Give your partner a secret test.* Your insecurities about everything cause you to find ways to see if your partner really cares or not. Naturally, your partner almost always fails because he or she has no idea that there is a test in the first place.
- ▲ *Fight dirty.* Fighting with you is like being in a street fight. Not only do you erupt like a volcano but you curse, name call, and insult everyone within a two-mile radius. A few minutes later and it's all over. You feel fine, but your partner is left dazed and confused.
- ▲ *Maintain the "You did to me so I'll do it to you" cycle.* For you getting back at your partner is justifiable. Even though your husband couldn't go to your office party because he had to work late, you won't go to his party. Just because your wife forgot to fill the gas tank, you'll do the same even though she has an early office meeting.

- *Talk about your relationship with everyone from your mother to your yoga instructor.* You talk to everyone about everything. You're constantly gathering opinions and advice from outsiders. Eventually you have so many conflicting opinions that you don't know what to do.
- *Agree that you're going to do something—and then don't.* After a long heart-to-heart talk with your spouse, you both agree that it's time for you to take care of the family finances. Despite your good intentions, the bills are put off, and eventually you and your partner are having the same argument again.
- *Become the complainer.* You're the person who is never happy because nothing is ever right—enough. The restaurant's air conditioning is too cold, the menu too boring, and the service too slow.
- *Keep changing the subject during an argument.* Fighting with you is like trying to catch a fish with bare hands. One minute you're arguing about the lawn and in the next you're bringing up that incident with your mother-in-law 20 years ago. Before long nothing gets resolved and you can't remember what got you mad in the first place.

Infidelity: The Cheating Heart

Infidelity is a painful event in any marriage and in a league all its own when it comes to the turmoil, mistrust, and resentment it provokes. Those who have gone through it describe it as one of the most agonizing experiences of their life.

For years researchers have tried to get accurate statistics on infidelity in a marriage. Some experts estimate that 60 percent of husbands and 40 percent of wives will have an affair during their marriage (*The Monogamy Myth* by Peggy Vaughn). The ironic thing is that people tend to be less than totally honest on this subject for two contradictory reasons. The first reason is shame and guilt. The experience has been so excruciating that even if it's an anonymous poll, the individual still won't acknowledge it. It is more comfortable and less dishonorable to deny the whole thing. On the other hand, there are those who like to "talk the talk" and exaggerate about his or her conquests. Apparently, embellishing the truth makes them feel more powerful or attractive.

Unlike a terrible argument, it is nearly impossible to keep the lid on infidelity. The news about someone cheating moves faster than a brush fire. The impact is felt outside the couple, to their children, parents, family, friends, and colleagues. People take sides. Friendships dissolve.

Is infidelity a death sentence for a marriage? As traumatic as it is, many family therapists describe that a couple can heal and move forward. Marriage expert Michele Weiner-Davis, author of *Divorce Busting* (M. Weiner-Davis, 1993) and *The Divorce Remedy,* (M. Weiner-Davis, 2001), states that most marriages survive infidelity. Weiner-Davis warns that although couples can survive, it is how they survive that is most important.

The road to salvaging a marriage after a partner has strayed is hard and takes a lot of rebuilding, but these steps may make the healing possible:

- ▲ *Open up and be honest.* Infidelity is not something to sweep under the rug. It needs to be talked about honestly and in depth. The person who has been cheated on has the right to know the details of the affair. They need to be able to ask questions and to know all the facts. On the other hand, the person who has been unfaithful needs to be able to express the reasons why it happened. There are many reasons why a person has an affair. As painful as these talks might be, it's the only way to start to heal if you plan to stay married.
- ▲ *The affair needs to be over.* As obvious as that may sound, an affair must come to an end if you intend to restore your marriage. How can two people rebuild trust and commitment if one continues to see someone else? Don't fool yourself or expect your partner to understand that you've ended the relationship as "friends" and continue to talk on the phone or have coffee together.
- ▲ *Spend time together.* As important as it is to be open and discuss the infidelity, it is equally important to spend healing time together. While you're trying to mend the relationship, make time to relax and have some fun together. Take a walk on the beach. Ride your bicycles. It doesn't have to cost a dime, just spend time together.

Don't be ashamed if you find that getting through this period is more than you can handle. If you and your partner can't talk without it leading

Contact ***The American Association for Marriage and Family Therapy*** *(AAMFT) at www.amft.org if you are looking for a therapist in the U.S., Canada, or overseas. The AAMFT provides a helpful site called Therapist Locator.net that offers the names and backgrounds of over 15,000 family and marriage therapists.*

to tears and an argument, then consider seeking the help of a family and marriage therapist.

The Titanic

Sometimes no matter how hard you try, a marriage ends in divorce. In fact, according to a report from the CDC, about 43 percent of first marriages end in separation or divorce within 15 years. The reasons why a marriage ends can be as varied as the couples themselves. How do you know when you're on a sinking ship without any hope for recovery? Some people linger for years, even decades, in unhappy relationships before they realize that the situation is hopeless. Consider these red flags if you are uncertain whether or not to stay in your marriage.

- There is physical, mental, or emotional abuse.
- There is chronic adultery.
- You spend more and more time imagining what your life would be like without your partner.
- You're indifferent from years of stored up resentment, hurt, or frustration and no longer have the energy or desire to work at the marriage anymore.
- You don't respect or admire your partner.
- You feel as if you're suffocating in mud and if you don't leave you'll get sick or die.

Why Do I *Always* Have To Be the One to Change?

Have you ever felt that way? As if you're the only one who's noticing the problems and willing to do something about it? You feel as if all your talking, prodding, and pleading is falling on deaf ears. The notion that you should have to do yet one more thing to turn this marriage around is too much to contemplate.

The truth is that you shouldn't *always* have to be the one to change. It doesn't seem fair, but maybe you should be the one to initiate change. The reason is simple. You do it for yourself. You deserve to be happy and more fulfilled. If that means you taking charge of the situation—so be it. One thing's for sure, if you continue to wait, it's likely that nothing is going to change. You'll continue to feel as if you are stuck in the mud. Ask yourself these questions:

What relationship issues keep repeating over and over in your marriage?

1. ______________________________
2. ______________________________
3. ______________________________
4. ______________________________
5. ______________________________

What is your typical way of handling these concerns?

1. ______________________________
2. ______________________________
3. ______________________________
4. ______________________________
5. ______________________________

How would your partner say you usually handle these concerns?

1. ______________________________
2. ______________________________
3. ______________________________
4. ______________________________
5. ______________________________

Now take a moment and consider your relationship goals. Once again, keep in mind that to get where you want to go, you first need to know where you are going.

Write down your top five goals toward having a more fulfilling marriage:

1. ______________________________
2. ______________________________
3. ______________________________
4. ______________________________
5. ______________________________

Now ask yourself this question:

On a scale ranging from 1 to 10, with 1 being "the worst" and 10 being "great," how well would you say you are taking care of your marriage right now?

____

____

If you answered with a 9 or 10, well done. But before you get a swelled head remember that there are highs and lows in any relationship. Just when you think you can relax and coast for a while, life has a way of knocking that smile right off your face.

How have you managed to keep a strong marriage so far? What is working for you?

____

____

____

What could you do to bring your score up half a notch, say to a 9½? If you gave yourself a 10, what can you continue to do to keep your score at a ten?

____

____

____

____

If you find that your scores are on the low side, then ask yourself this question:

What kinds of things have you been doing to keep your score at a two or five? Think about it—you didn't give yourself a zero so you must be doing a few things correctly. What have you managed to do right?

____

____

____

____

If you are thinking that with scores this low the marriage is hopeless, you're wrong. If you didn't give yourself a big, round zero, it's because you have noticed a few positive signs in your marriage.

What if you can find nothing nice to say about your marriage? Think smaller.

What is one more small thing you can do in your marriage to bring your score up a point?

____

____

____

What will do you do to ensure that you keep doing that one small thing?

How will your life be different when you manage to get your score up a few points?

What will you be doing that you are not doing now?

Who will be the most surprised about these positive changes?

What a Good Marriage Looks Like

Let's face it, we're all human beings with different beliefs, perceptions, and experiences. That said, no two couples are exactly alike. Furthermore, there is no *one* way for a couple to act to have a good marriage. However, there are common elements found in the foundations of the strongest marriages:

- *The couple respects each other.* Partners in a strong and satisfying marriage find important ways to respect the other. It may be the way that one handles the children, juggles a hectic work schedule, makes money, or is a gourmet cook.

- *The couple is tolerant of each other.* These couples are more realistic with one another. Sure, they don't like the fact that their partner is always late, makes a mess in the kitchen, or always seems to be checking his or her stocks online—but they can tolerate that.
- *Each partner wishes to accentuate the positive and eliminate the negative.* In other words, each spouse wishes to make the most of the marriage assets while minimizing its flaws. These couples take a more positive outlook toward their marriage. They prefer to value and appreciate what's working than to focus in on what's not working.

Start by Breaking All the Rules

The relationship between two people cannot be in balance all the time. There are moments when one partner needs more and the other must answer the call. The happiest couples are those who not only focus on their relationship, they protect it. They are sensitive to the rhythm of the marriage and ignore the myths and opinions of others.

Marriage can be the ultimate tightrope walk. The road to maintaining balance in your marriage is to let go of your expectations and beliefs about what it all should be like. Don't be afraid to break the rules and do what's right in your relationship. Success comes from looking at what works and doing more of it.

CHAPTER 8

BALANCE WITH CHILDREN AND FAMILIES: THE TIGHTROPE GETS CROWDED

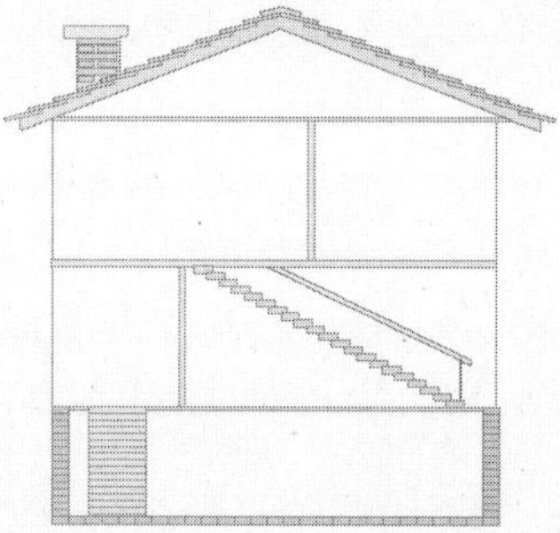

Nothing can upset your sense of balance during your day more than *that* call. Which one? Well, take your pick. The one in which your child's teacher delivers the news that your teenage daughter has neglected to turn in her science fair project and will receive a "D" for the semester. The one in which your child's day care teacher calls and says your daughter bit a playmate—or was on the receiving end of a bite and now has a big welt.

When you go home, more balance issues can arise. Your wife has promised the kids pizza and a video and you believe they need to hit the books. Your husband has handed your daughter 20 dollars for the movies again—when you told her she couldn't go until she cleaned her room.

Children and family issues strike at the very heart of our values and dreams—it's no wonder we react with such passion when issues with our kids arise. Here are some typical scenarios that affect our sense of balance in our families.

- ▲ You and your spouse have vastly different parenting styles. Even the best of marriages are in for an awakening when that little bundle of joy arrives. One spouse may be indulgent; the other the disciplinarian.

One may believe only organic foods should pass through a baby's lips; the other may be taking them for their first Happy Meal before their second birthday. Arguments can arise over everything from clothes and food to discipline and even religion.

- ▲ Children take center stage and a couple forgets to nurture each other *as* a couple.
- ▲ The issues of today's teens, from drugs to school violence to early sexual experiences, leave parents frightened, stressed, and unsure of how to navigate the territory of hormones and slammed bedroom doors.
- ▲ A child may have a serious issue, such as a learning disability, illness, or bullies at school, and this places a strain on the couple.
- ▲ The simple stress and complexity of modern life with two working parents means exhaustion, guilt, and lack of quality time with children.
- ▲ One parent is the wage earner and one stays at home and tension arises from this situation.
- ▲ Divorce further complicates issues of child rearing.
- ▲ Blended families don't often resemble the Brady Bunch—they're more like MTV's "The Real World"—and have their own difficult balancing act bringing together a new couple and their assorted children.
- ▲ Finally, there are other common complex family issues from aging parents to in-laws that may not have to do with parenthood but still have everything to do with stress and impinging on our lives and sense of balance.

Balance is needed when walking the tightrope with children and families . . . but this issue is an emotional hot button and often hard to arrive at a sense of serenity over. There is hope, however, by following our program of clear thinking and goal setting.

Applying very clear thinking can help to make the problems of raising a family and family issues seem less mountainous. We're the first to admit that often we're outnumbered. Erica has three kids ranging in ages from

5 to 13—and each age brings with it its own unique problems. But clear thinking can help break things down into manageable chunks.

Instead of Fuzzy Thinking	Think Cearly
I want to spend quality time with my kids. →	I will set aside one night this week as "family night," turn off the phones, order pizza, and talk and play board games.
I will try to get my spouse and I to agree on discipline procedures. →	This week my spouse and I will go out alone without the children to discuss a discipline plan we can both agree on. If we have trouble deciding on a plan, we will at least find one or two ideas we can both agree to use and try.
I will spend more quality time with my spouse. →	My spouse and I will hire a babysitter this week for a date night. We will designate at least 15 minutes to "not talking about the kids."

The idea of fuzzy versus clear thinking, again, is to take some measurable action. It isn't enough to "want" to be rid of something or to "want" something as vague and unmeasurable as "quality time." What the heck does that buzz word mean anyway?

We are all victims of the media and television when it comes to families. Why does it seem that sitcom families always seem to be able to sit down for dinner together every night? All arguments are resolved in half an hour (less commercial time). Meddlesome in-laws, like the Marie character on "Everybody Loves Raymond," still really love their children (though personally, if we were Deborah, we would have killed her already!) and you never doubt that. There isn't the level of poison you can sometimes see in families with toxic issues. "Quality time," therefore, is what you make of it. Quality time may not bring to mind images of watching TV together, but we know a family that rents videos on family night, makes popcorn, and all have a good cuddle and hang-out in the den. Don't let others define what it is you want your family to look like. You can find yourself extremely out of balance trying to live up to a media image more appropriate to Mayberry R. F. D. than today's modern family. If you're okay with your teen piercing her belly button and dying her hair because she's in a phase, and yet that same teen is the one who tells you *everything*, then don't worry that you don't look like The Cosbys or The Bradys. It's sometimes okay to look like The Osbournes.

Write Your Own Map

Now it's time to write that map. Personally, our own ideal of family doesn't include food shoveled down in the car en route to soccer practice or days of work so exhausted that it leaves us snapping at our children at night. This probably isn't anyone's ideal. But now is the time to get at the heart of what you really *do* want.

What are your goals as far as your family life? (Remember to be specific and measurable.) What family issues would you like to resolve?

1. ____
2. ____
3. ____
4. ____
5. ____

This next part is important. Imagine for a moment that you have accomplished everything on your family balance list. Answer this question:

What will your life be like when you have achieved your family goals? What will it mean to you to have this balance in your home?

____

____

____

____

____

____

What will be the smallest sign that you are moving in the right direction and that your family is starting to transform to one that is more balanced? You want to list this sign so that you can see your progress and recognize it.

____

____

When there is a positive change in one area, other positive changes will occur somewhere else. If you think of life as walking that tightrope, the balancing act is an art form unto itself. When you add multiple players on the highwire act, it's no wonder it can wobble. The good news is that if your marriage is more balanced, for instance, your childrearing will go more smoothly. If you have your spirituality more balanced (see Chapter 11), the next time you hear that one of your teen's best friends has had a scrape with the law or your teen starts asking about birth control, you can center yourself first and then react. Balancing your life means coping with all the areas in a more centered and peaceful way.

The Big Ones

We all have times when everything seems to go wrong in our families. We're under the gun at work, which is the worst possible time for things to be going wrong at home—but you know they are. Your spouse is on edge from layoffs at his or her corporation, and the kids, seeming to pick up on the tension, have become miniature monsters. You barely recognize them for their fangs! They are acting up at school and your teen has decided to press that issue of the belly button piercing. In addition, your paycheck is just *barely* covering your living expenses, you're not saving enough for college, and now your son wants to join a travel hockey team, meaning a big outlay of dollars. But in reality, in modern life, this is a pretty common scenario. Add into the mix 150 emails a day, your cell phone ringing at all hours, and a little technological stress.

But there are also "big issues." We can joke and be playful with some of the scenarios we've outlined—mostly because we ourselves have been victims of them. In our last book we shared about little ones covering the dog in Post-its, or the time Kathy's kids stripped naked and danced on the front lawn while she was trying to do a *live* radio interview. But there are some issues we just can't joke about and these are the ones that can throw you for such a loop you're left gasping—a teen experimenting with drugs, a child withdrawing into a deep depression, or a mother-in-law who drinks enough to be unsafe around the children. There's no parenting manual for some of these big issues, and in truth, if you are facing a crisis of very large proportions, you may find that it's time to consult a therapist.

Big or small, though, list the five most pressing crises you're facing—the ones that really press in on your sense of balance.

1. ______________________________
2. ______________________________
3. ______________________________
4. ______________________________
5. ______________________________

Now it is time to set small measurable steps to achieve balance in these areas.

Too Big	**Just Right**
I will get along with my mother-in-law.	I will make sure she isn't alone with the kids when she is drinking heavily. Today I will refrain from making snide comments about her alcohol consumption.
I will get along with my moody teen.	I will NOT comment about her hair. No matter how much I hate blue.
I will stop reacting when my kids don't do their chores.	I will make a chore list and make sure each child does ONE thing today.

By taking steps that are small and measurable, you can feel a sense of accomplishment.

OUTSIDE THE BOX

Erica—My life is about as insane as they come . . . I have three kids in varying ages and though each only does ONE activity, that's three activities and three schedules. One thing I did to find some balance was to be certain we have some weekend days when we plan NOTHING. I do not have to be a one-woman cruise director and all three of my kids can entertain themselves without having to be entertained by ME.

Kathy—On any given day I feel like I'm locked in a cage with howler monkeys. Don't get me wrong, I love and adore my two children, but some days can take me to my last raw nerve. For me, the fast track to a tension headache is my 85-year-old mother in the front seat and my six- and nine-year-old in the back. She's hard of hearing and my son never stops talking. They both talk to me at the same time. When I answer his questions she thinks I'm saying something to her. "Sushi? I don't want any sushi? Why are you talking to me about sushi? I don't eat that stuff." I don't know how I haven't driven into a telephone pole. Believe it or not, what settles the natives are books-on-tape. When I drop a story CD in everyone seems to quiet down and listen. A miracle.

Ready to Begin Finding Your Balance?

Now it's time to balance your world with clear ideas of your goals in the family area.

Write down your top five goals toward your family.

1. ____________________
2. ____________________
3. ____________________
4. ____________________
5. ____________________

Now ask yourself this question:

On a scale of ranging from 1 to 10, with one being "the worst" and 10 being "great," how well would you say you are taking care of your family goals right now?

____

____

If you answered with a 9 or 10, that's impressive. But stick around because there is always more to learn. Remember that life has a way of throwing you a curve ball just when you think you have it all together.

How have you managed to maintain your sense of balance in this area so far? What is working for you? *(Give yourself some well-deserved credit!)*

____

____

____

What could you do to bring your score up half a notch, say to a 9½? If you gave yourself a 10, what can you continue to do to keep your score at a 10?

____

____

____

____

If feel like your family is completely out of control, chances are there are still some things you are doing right.

What kinds of things have you been doing to keep your score at a two or five? Think about it—you didn't give yourself a zero so you must be doing a few things correctly. What have you managed to do right?

If you are thinking that there simply couldn't be anything in a score that low, you're wrong. If you didn't give yourself a flat zero it is because in some small ways you are doing a few positive things to manage your family. Maybe you never send them to bed without a bedtime story. Maybe you're sure, even on your most hectic days, to be certain you tell them they are unconditionally loved.

What is one more thing you can do to find balance in your family life and bring your score up a point?

What will do you do to ensure that you keep doing that one small thing?

How will your life be different when you manage to get your score up a few points?

What will you be doing that you are not doing now?

Who will be the most surprised about these positive changes?

____

____

____

Changing the Past

One note about families of origins: In our chapter on emotional baggage, we discuss families of origin that have burdened us with old wounds. Just remember that the sins of the past needn't be repeated in the present. If you want to see an interesting conversation, the next time you are among *close* friends with men present of a certain age (40 to 45 or older), ask the question: *When was the last time your father told you he loved you?* The conversation may surprise you—and may be quite poignant. Times have changed. Many of our fathers never changed a diaper. Many of our mothers never worked outside the home. Many of us come to parenthood with a "map" that was totally different from the one we are living with now.

Some of us come with even darker issues. We are so bound and determined not to make the mistakes of our parents that we stress ourselves out trying to be "perfect." Well, guess what? There is no such thing as a perfect parent. There is no more admirable goal than to want to do the job of parenting well, but you can veer off the map that was written for you in childhood and write your own new map. And give yourself permission to make mistakes along the way.

The Wire of Parenthood

Watch your children sleeping to bring you to your knees with the power of unconditional love. It's humbling. Yet divorce, modern-day pressures, and the stress of being a wage-earner can make walking the tightrope of parenthood the one area we often feel we are working without a net. Have you ever snapped at a child who only wanted to ask you a simple question? That crest-fallen face can make you feel like you've been stabbed. So we want to walk that high-wire with grace. Know, simply, that as you set the goals for balance, you are like millions of parents across the country who are struggling to parent while coping with a pace more hectic than any other time in our history. The most important thing you will ever do has nothing to do with a gold plaque and a corner office, but when your children take their places in the world with decency, grace, and the confidence from having been raised with love.

CHAPTER 9

THE BALANCE OF FRIENDSHIP

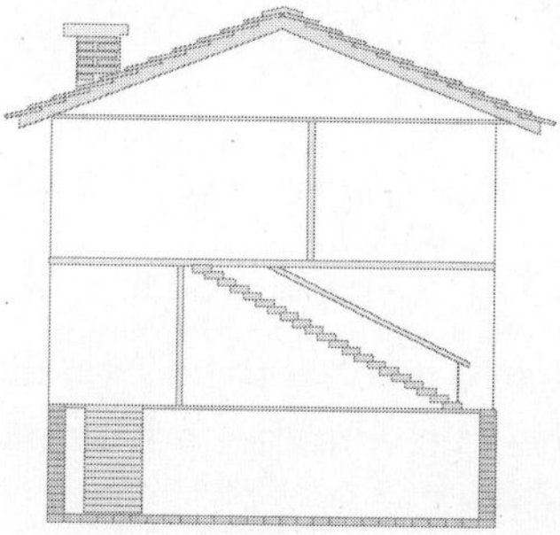

As valuable as friendship is, it may be one of the more overlooked areas of our lives. It is the one aspect of ourselves that we all need, but which we may take for granted. More often than not, it is a friend who helps you to get your life back into perspective when it's out of balance with the rest of the world.

One of the wonderful aspects of friendship is that unlike your family, you can pick your own friends. Face it—many of us have terrific families with close, satisfying relationships. But not everyone is that fortunate. Some people look around their family tree and say, "Tell me again how I ended up with these folks." Unlike family ties, a strong friendship allows you to be yourself, warts and all, without any thought of how you may be judged or viewed. Whether it's music, sports, education, or anything else, you can choose the friends with whom you share common interests.

According to RealAge.com, a long-term relationship can reduce a person's "Real-Age" by as much as six and a half years (www.entertainmates.com, July 27, 2003).

Why do we need friends, you may be asking? According to Jan Yager, friendship expert and author of *Friendshifts* (1999) and the best-selling

When Friendship Hurts (1999), friends are essential for our emotional well-being. Friends reduce the stress in our lives just by being there to talk and to get through life's unexpected curve balls. Researchers say that friends extend our lives as well as improve the quality of our lives. Friends will:

- ▲ Make you laugh at yourself.
- ▲ Make you feel loved when you've got a broken heart.
- ▲ Commiserate with you when you've had your 400th argument with your parents.
- ▲ Be honest enough to tell you what you were really like at that party the night before.
- ▲ Get out of bed at 3 a.m. to rescue you from a "situation."
- ▲ Give you the courage to go back to college, ask for a raise, move cross country, or break up with that jerk who you knew was no good for you in the first place.
- ▲ Tell you what you really look like in those pants.

Friendship, like all the things we treasure in our lives, requires some cultivation to keep it going strong. Throughout the course of this book, we encourage all of our readers to get your ideas and thoughts out of your head and into the light of day. Put them down on paper where you can take a good hard look and mull them over carefully. You may have to take a leap of faith and simply trust us when we tell you that everything looks different in black and white. We have a hunch that you will discover there is more going on in your friendships that feels right than feels wrong. It only takes one "thorn" to make you uncomfortable. If there is a thorn sticking in your side, there are constructive ways to change that.

What is the best part of your friendships? What aspects of your friendships do you value and consider assets?

1. ______________________________
2. ______________________________
3. ______________________________

4. ____________________
5. ____________________

From time to time, there are aspects of our friendships that feel uncomfortable or troubling. The balance feels off. Consider the question that follows:

What aspects of your friendships would you like to change? What are the concerns that have been wearing you down?

1. ____________________
2. ____________________
3. ____________________
4. ____________________
5. ____________________

In each and every chapter we talk about thinking styles—fuzzy versus clear. We believe that it bears repeating because the best way to lose your way is have no clue where you're going in the first place. If you're wondering how that applies to your friendships, consider this: Suppose you make the sweeping statement, "I feel like I'm in a rut with my friends." How does that statement inform you as to what you should do about it? The truth is that the statement mirrors how you feel, but provides no direction in which to solve your concern. For any change to occur in your life, you need to know where to begin, take small steps, and be able to recognize the signs that indicate you are on your way.

Instead of Fuzzy Thinking	Think Clearly
I need more friends. →	I will ask someone I feel comfortable with to join me for coffee.
I've got to get back in touch with my friends, but my life is so hectic. →	This week I will send out a brief note or email to two friends that I haven't spoken to in a while.

Breaking the Ice

Have you ever found yourself in a large group of people and you didn't know a soul? You feel self-conscious, as if you've just realized that you're wearing your underwear over your clothes. Everybody's mingling, laughing, and swapping great stories about their successful lives. And there you are, well, just standing there.

Breaking the ice to make conversation with people you don't know feels awkward because you have to climb out from your comfortable place and extend yourself. What if they don't like you or don't find you interesting? What if you have a big piece of spinach stuck in your teeth? After all, you don't know anyone, what can you possibly say or have in common?

Even though breaking the ice may initially feel uncomfortable, the potential rewards are worth the effort. The biggest reward is friendship. New friends are everywhere if you open yourself up to the possibilities.

Let's get back to you at the cocktail party. You want to approach the other guests to start a conversation, but aren't sure how to get started. Conversation expert, Chris Widener, makes the following suggestions: Get people to talk about themselves by asking questions. Listen for what you may have in common and go after those connections.

Except for the rare exception, most people like to talk about themselves. After all, it is the subject they know best. The more you get people to talk about themselves, the more likely it is that they will remember you not only as a great listener, but as an interesting person. When it's time to move on, simply say, "It's been nice talking with you. Enjoy the rest of the evening." If it's a business function or if you've made a professional connection you might want to pass your business card along. If you feel as if this is someone you could meet for coffee, play golf with, or visit, then by all means, exchange phone numbers.

OUTSIDE THE BOX

Kathy—I have the good fortune of having some very good friends, Erica being one of them. In my house, friends are like family. Like family, we are together through thick and thin. My friends are a diverse group and not necessarily a mirror reflection of me. A wise friend once told me that lasting friendships are built on concessions. If you have a friend that's always late, then she or he is your late friend. You don't force him or her to change. I took those words to heart and seldom have disagreements with any of my friends. Likewise, they don't have disagreements with me. Our friendship is what's important.

Erica—Kathy operates on "Kathy Time," and so we all know what's going on in the previous paragraph! In terms of balance, I sincerely believe you can count your close friends on one hand, after which you fan out into casual friends and acquaintances. My closest friends are the people I can call to say I have had not just a bad day, but a day of such epic proportions of horribleness that if I am not in possession of a martini soon, I am going to go lock myself in a closet. Because my five closest friends also know I am claustrophobic, they listen to this with bemusement. In all seriousness, though, if your weekends and social calendar are a whirlwind of keeping up with "social commitments," it may be time to whittle your "must see" list to those friends who really will arrive with martini shaker in hand and a good joke to boost your spirits.

Write Your Own Map

If you are interested in making friendships or improving the quality of your friendships, then it's time to make a plan.

Instead of Saying	Say
I want to meet interesting people. →	I am going to join a community theater group.
I'm tired of just hanging out every weekend. →	I am going to talk with my friends about putting some short weekend trips on our calendar.

This is the right time to consider what you need in your friendships. This isn't the right time to jot down all the things that irk you about your friends.

What are your goals for your friendships? (Remember to be specific and measurable.) What concerns would you like to resolve?

1. ______________________________
2. ______________________________
3. ______________________________
4. ______________________________
5. ______________________________

Don't fly over this next section. Imagine for a moment that you have accomplished everything on your friendship list. Now answer this question:

What will your life be like when these concerns no longer affect your friendships? What will you be doing? What will you be enjoying that are not enjoying at this moment?

1. ______________________________
2. ______________________________
3. ______________________________
4. ______________________________
5. ______________________________

Finally, take another moment and consider this next question about looking for small signs. The signs you notice along the way will encourage and motivate you to keep on your path to change.

What will be the smallest signs that you are moving in the right direction and away from those aspects of your friendships that have frustrated or disappointed you? Remember—think small.

1. ______________________________
2. ______________________________
3. ______________________________
4. ______________________________
5. ______________________________

We cannot emphasize enough the importance of thinking small. Small is doable and more likely to succeed.

Think Big	Just Right
I'm going to be a better friend. →	I'm going to invite a few friends over for pizza and a movie this weekend.
I'm going to be more outgoing at parties.	I will introduce myself to two people.

Kick Your Friendships Up a Notch

Like anything else, friendships can fall into a rut. Every weekend it's the same old same old. Maybe you have old friends you've been meaning to contact, but never get around to it. Then again, maybe you would like to break out of your mold and make new friends. Here's a few quick suggestions:

- ▲ Step outside your box and do something completely different—join a theater group, wine tasting group, karate studio, cycling club, or reading group. The list of possibilities are endless, but the point is to just "do it."
- ▲ Buy season tickets to the ballet, opera, or the theater. If cultural events don't excite you then look into something that does. Maybe it's basketball, ice-skating, or even wrestling. Take a different friend every time or bring a business associate.

- ▲ Get a group of friends together and have a cooking party. Invite one of the local chefs to your home and have him or her give the group a lesson.
- ▲ Invite a dance instructor to your home to give you and your friends a few dance lessons.
- ▲ Sit down with your friends and put some fun weekends on the calendar.
- ▲ For something completely different, look into something bigger like going on a sailing or fishing trip, or even space camp.
- ▲ Start a readers group with your friends.
- ▲ Pick an important cause in your community and organize a few of your friends to do something about it.
- ▲ Join the local gym or YMCA with your friends and go together.
- ▲ Start a basketball, tennis, soccer, volleyball, or softball league.
- ▲ Take an art, photography, or sculpting class with a group of friends.

What relationship issues keep repeating over and over in your friendships?

1. ______________________________
2. ______________________________
3. ______________________________
4. ______________________________
5. ______________________________

What is your typical way of handling these concerns?

1. ______________________________
2. ______________________________
3. ______________________________
4. ______________________________
5. ______________________________

How would my friends say I usually handle these concerns?

1. ____________________
2. ____________________
3. ____________________
4. ____________________
5. ____________________

Take some time and think about your friendship goals. Once again, keep in mind that to get where you want to go, you first need to know where you are going.

Write down your top five goals toward having more satisfying friendships.

1. ____________________
2. ____________________
3. ____________________
4. ____________________
5. ____________________

Now ask yourself this question:

On a scale ranging from 1 to 10, with 1 being "the worst" and 10 being "great," how well would you say you are taking care of your friendships right now?

____

____

How have you managed to keep strong friendships so far? What is working for you?

____

____

____

What could you do to bring your score up half a notch, say to 9½? If you gave yourself a 10, what can you continue to do to keep your score at a 10?

____

____

____

If you notice that your scores are on the low end, then ask yourself this question:

What kinds of things have you been doing to keep your score at a two or five? Think about it—you didn't give yourself a zero so you must be doing a few things correctly. What have you managed to do right?

____

____

____

____

If you're coming to the conclusion that with scores this low you'll end up without a friend in the world, you're wrong. If you didn't write down a zero, maybe it's because you have realized that there are a few redeeming signs about your friendships.

What's that, you say? You can't find anything to say about any of your friendships? Then think smaller.

What is one more small thing you can do in your friendships to bring your score up a point?

____

____

____

What will you do to ensure that you keep doing that one small thing?

____

____

____

How will your life be different when you manage to get your score up a few points?

____

____

____

What will you be doing that you are not doing now?

____

____

____

Who will be the most surprised about these positive changes?

____

____

____

How True Blue Are You?

When you look around at the quality of your friendships, you must also ask yourself how true blue are you? Are you a desirable friend? Maintaining the balance in friendship is a two-way street. You have to give to receive. Is it possible that your friendships feel off because you've been taking them for granted or not doing your share? Ask yourself these questions:

1. When a friend calls, do you call them back in a reasonable amount of time?
2. When a friend's in trouble, do you go to his or her aid?
3. Do you talk about your friends to other people?
4. Do you begrudge friends their success?
5. Can you keep a promise? How about a secret?
6. When your friend is in trouble, does he or she come to you for advice?
7. When a friend is upset with you can you talk about it?
8. If you were in a bind, would you turn to a friend like you for assistance?
9. Are you critical when a friend takes a risk or tries something new?
10. How often do you get into arguments with your friends?

As our culture changes and grows, friendship will become more important in our lives. Fifty years ago, people tended to stay in the area where they were raised. Not so today. Today families are spread out not only across the country but all around the world. Although you cannot replace family members, friendships are filling those voids and becoming more and more important.

You can walk the tightrope of life alone, but it sure is a lot more fun with friends at your side. Like you, your friends face daily struggles and setbacks. Like you, they will experience both success and loss. Keeping your toes firmly upon the tightrope means being the best friend you can be.

CHAPTER 10

BALANCING IN COMMUNITY: VOLUNTEERING AND YOUR PLACE IN THE WORLD

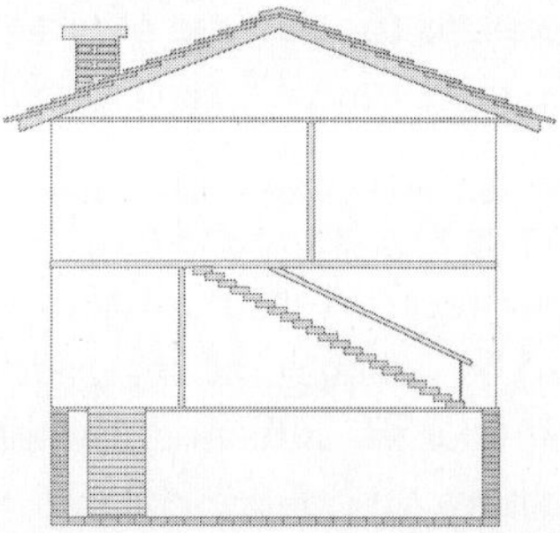

When your life is stretched so thin, the thought of volunteering or doing good works within your community at large may be the furthest thing from your mind. "If I can't even find enough hours in the day to get my 'to-do' list done, how am I going to find time to volunteer?"

Yet, for many, there may be an internal "calling" to volunteer. You may see an ad on television for the Boys & Girls Clubs of America or you may get a note home from your kids' school asking about tutoring kids who are having trouble reading. You may look around your neighborhood or community and see some very pressing needs—homelessness, neighborhood blight, teens with no place to hang out. Maybe you want to volunteer for more global issues like social justice. But you wonder if you have the time. When contemplating volunteering, consider the following:

- Volunteering is almost universally considered, by those who do it, an integral part of their lives. Most call it "enriching" and "rewarding."
- Ralph Waldo Emerson once said that success is marked by leaving the world a better place, whether by a "healthy child, a garden patch, or a redeemed social condition." Volunteering can include activities large and small.

- ▲ Volunteering can be an hour a week doing something as simple as cleaning the altar of your church or doing gardening work at your synagogue or place of worship, or it can be as extensive as becoming certified as a CASA (Court Appointed Special Advocate) for an abused child.
- ▲ Most volunteers feel they get more from the volunteering than they put into it.
- ▲ As the Baby Boomers age, there may be a sense of wanting to make a difference in a real way, as the passage of time becomes more clear and real. Volunteering is a way of feeling useful, vibrant, and relevant.

Okay, so you're running in a thousand directions. How and when will you find the time to volunteer? Well, if you're restoring some balance to your "house," you should be seeing some things settle down. There is also a question of prioritizing your volunteering. By this we mean that sometimes, particularly if you have school-age children, you will be asked to sell popcorn for Scouting or magazines for the school library, come in to make copies for the teacher, spend weekends helping out the soccer team, coach two sports, bake cookies for the church bake sale . . . you get the idea. But is this the kind of volunteering you *want* to be doing or are you starting to become a victim of "volunteer burnout"? If the answer is that all this is making you dizzy, then learn a very powerful two-letter word: NO! And stick to it. This doesn't make you a terrible person or a terrible parent. Obtaining a life in balance is about setting priorities that work for you—which is the perfect way to express yourself to others. "No . . . I am prioritizing my life and right now, this doesn't work for me." End of story. Don't be bullied or goaded into it (unless this is what you want to do). Next, you need to use our clear thinking techniques to figure out what you want to do as a volunteer.

Instead of Fuzzy Thinking	Think Clearly
I want to volunteer for several "important" causes. →	I will spend some time clearly thinking about my priorities and find one cause I believe in passionately to give my time to.

Instead of Fuzzy Thinking	Think Clearly
I will do as much as I can for my cause. →	I will start with a small commitment, see how that works in my life, and then build from there. An hour a week might work for me to start. I need both passion for a cause AND boundaries.

Write Your Own Map: Defining Your Passions in Volunteering

If you now feel as if making time for volunteering or finding a place of balance in your life where you can contribute to your community is important, where do you begin? First, it might help to come up with some ideas for the broad types of causes that you feel are important to you. Is it the well-being of kids and teens? Homelessness? Helping alcoholics or victims of domestic violence? Manning a suicide hotline? Helping your church or place of worship? Helping the nation's schools? Wildlife preservation?

Next try plugging in "Volunteering" in a search engine, or read your local paper, which often has free ads for local charities and organizations needing help.

Then, when you have narrowed down your choices, "interview" the organizations you find interesting. For instance, how long has the charity been in existence? How much of its budget actually gets into the hands of those in need? What is the annual salary of the CEO? Frankly, if it's in the half a million dollar range, we think that's offensive for a charitable organization! If it's a smaller scale organization, you can ask how hands-on your experiences will be. Once you've made your choice, you will likely either receive some training or a background check, depending on the work you choose to do. To mentor teens, Erica had to be fingerprinted and checked out by the FBI. Thank goodness that old bank robbery didn't show up!

OUTSIDE THE BOX

Erica—I have always been a volunteer. I tutored Cambodian and Vietnamese refugees in English as a Second Language for years. Now I am a mentor to an unwed teen mother. This doesn't mean I don't have weeks in which I question my sanity about how I am going to get it all done, but somehow, at the end of the time I spend with my teen, I feel like I've been given a gift . . . and I feel surprisingly sane, though that may be debatable.

KATHY—Over the years I've tried as best as I can to reinforce the idea of doing for others with my two children. They have a good life and I want them to understand that not everyone is as fortunate. One of the proudest moments in my life occurred shortly after September 11. My then seven-year-old son Peter came to me and said, "Mom, I've got to do something for all those fire and policemen." I gave him a few ideas and stood back. Peter decided to have a bake sale and donate all the money to the World Trade Center fire and police funds. He set up the bake sale outside his aunt and uncle's deli. To Peter's surprise, a New York City fire marshal who had lost 18 friends on September 11 came to stand next to him. The fire marshal took his fire hat out of his car and placed it on Peter's head. People lined up to buy the cookies or just to make a donation. When it was over we drove Peter into the city and randomly picked a firehouse. Peter rang the station house bell and the huge door slowly rolled up. Inside the entrance were pictures of the firemen from that firehouse who lost their lives on September 11. Small votive candles burned under their photographs—eight strong, brave faces taken too soon. The firemen gathered around Peter to meet and thank him. After he handed his bake sale earnings over to the Captain, Peter wanted to go. On this day he wasn't interested in the trucks or the equipment. He seemed to know that there was a time for that, but not today. Today was for giving to those whose loss was bigger than anything we could ever imagine.

Now it's time to write your specific map.

What are your goals as far as volunteering? (Remember to be specific and measurable.) What causes would you like to help?

1. ______________________________
2. ______________________________
3. ______________________________
4. ______________________________
5. ______________________________

This next part is important. Imagine for a moment that you are a volunteer. Answer this question:

What will your life be like when you are doing some social good every week or month? How will volunteering change your life? How will it feel?

____

____

____

____

____

____

When there is a positive change in one area, other positive changes will occur somewhere else. If you restore some order into your work life, you may find volunteering is a new room in your house that feels fantastic. If you think of the house analogy, all the rooms work in conjunction. You don't build a house (unless you have a very funky architect) and set pods or separate rooms all over your land connected by tunnels, with no order, only chaos. If your marriage is in balance, you may feel that you do, indeed, have the time to make a difference. Just remember to do things in moderation.

Too Big	Just Right
I will run off with Greenpeace and save all the whales.→	This week I will contribute to a letter-writing campaign to my senator about the issues important to my cause.
I will work five days a week on my lunch hour at my child's school. →	I will speak to my child's teacher about one area I can help out in once a week or once every two weeks.

Try to avoid all or nothing thinking. Yes, there are some courageous and even foolhardy souls who place their lives on the line for causes in which they believe. But, if you get involved in small ways, you are still making a contribution, just as if you decline to sell popcorn and magazines and gift wrap and calendars, guess what? You are still a good mom or dad.

Ready to Volunteer?

Now it's time to balance your world with clear ideas of your goals regarding volunteering.

Write down your top five goals about volunteering, now that you have read this chapter.

1. ____
2. ____
3. ____
4. ____
5. ____

Now ask yourself this question:

On a scale ranging from 1 to 10, with 1 being "the worst," and 10 being "great," how well would you say you are taking care of your dreams and goals about volunteering right now?

____

____

If you answered with a 9 or 10, that's impressive. But you may find things falling out of balance at some other point in your life, remember that the balance game is NOT static. It is very much like the tightrope—full of little wobbles and almost invisible tremors of the rope.

How have you managed to maintain your sense of balance in this area so far? What is working for you? *(Give yourself some well-deserved credit!)*

____

____

____

What could you do to bring your score up half a notch, say to a 9½? If you gave yourself a 10, what can you continue to do to keep your score at a 10?

____

____

____

____

If you feel you have not been doing things in the volunteering arena well—or you feel you are volunteering, but not for the causes you want—look at that.

What kinds of things have you been doing to keep your score at a two or five? Think about it—you didn't give yourself a zero so you must be doing a few things correctly. What have you managed to do right?

____

____

____

____

If you are thinking that there simply couldn't be anything in a score that low, you're wrong. If you didn't give yourself a flat zero it is because in some small ways you are doing a few positive things to make a difference.

What is one more thing you can do to find balance in this area and bring your score up a point?

____

____

____

What will do you do to ensure that you keep doing that one small thing?

____

____

How will your life be different when you manage to get your score up a few points?

____

____

What will you be doing that you are not doing now?

____

____

Who will be the most surprised about these positive changes?

____

____

____

Beware of Burnout!

One final word about volunteering. It's no crime if a year from now you decide the cause you were once so passionate about no longer interests you. You may also get involved in an organization that from the outside looks great, but on the inside is full of infighting. Alternatively, you may be so good at what you do as a volunteer that you are taken advantage of. That is not good for your sense of balance. Erica was once a member of a very small church and taught Sunday school as well as ran a youth group. Although the new minister swore he would never allow volunteers to not be thanked, in fact, the more people did, the more that was expected of them, and the words "thank you" were never uttered. If you have an experience like this, don't let it sour you on volunteering. It's a noble pursuit, and there are literally thousands of organizations that can use your help.

CHAPTER 11

BALANCING LIFE WITH SPIRITUALITY

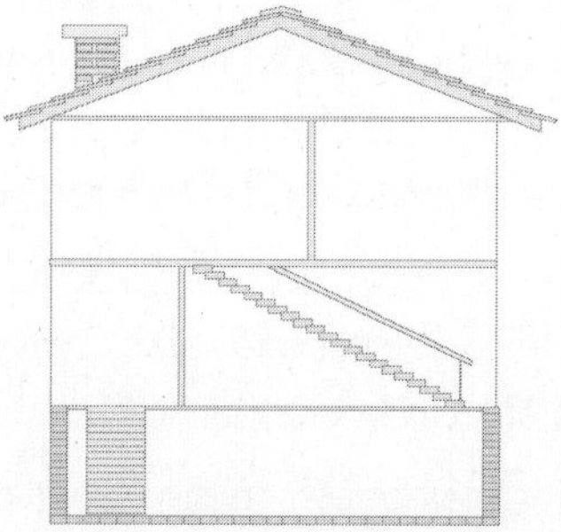

Many people find that their natural instinct is to turn to their spiritual foundation or religious beliefs when life finds them frazzled. Most of us believe that at our core is a spiritual essence or soul. Admittedly, when you have a day that sounds sort of like the following, you need *something*: You wake at 5:30 a.m., pack three lunches for each of your kids, fight over the shower schedule, your spouse takes one kid to daycare and two catch the bus. Before you are down the block starting your commute, your oldest child calls you on your cell phone and *begs* you to drop off her homework assignment at school so she doesn't flunk biology. You do this, followed by a one-hour commute in stop-and-go traffic, get to work to find an immediate crisis over a management report, wolf down lunch at your desk, get a call at 3:00 that the preschooler is throwing up at daycare, and call your spouse to fight over who is leaving work early to handle the situation. You flip a coin and lose. So, you go to daycare, bringing home a briefcase of work, and then you get your child settled on the couch with a video. You work from home until the dinner hour. Your spouse is taking your middle child to soccer. You eat take-out—and yours is cold because your sick child throws up in the middle of you trying to eat it. Laundry. Homework supervision. Baths for children. Check email. Another crisis looming at work. Vaguely kiss your spouse's cheek before passing out. Start whole thing all over again . . . Sound familiar?

It's not always fun being a grown-up. There . . . we said it. In fact, if anyone told us when we were kids what it's *really* like to be an adult, most of us would have opted to stay children forever. Maybe Peter Pan had the right idea. The aforementioned out-of-breath scenario doesn't even take into account some of the more common "big issue" problems such as the following.

- ▲ Being part of the "sandwich" generation, meaning you have both young children and aging parents to care for. Kathy's mother lived with her for a number of years and she had to contend with falls and medical crises. Both of us have young children ranging in age from 5 to 13.
- ▲ Financial pressures. The dollar doesn't go as far as it used to and the old ideal of being able to live on one salary has gone the same way as the fantasy of being able to live on Social Security after retirement.
- ▲ Company downsizing and layoffs mean departments have to get by with fewer people doing the work of more.
- ▲ Any kind of illness in yourself, friends, or family members.
- ▲ Lugging around emotional baggage (see Chapter 6).
- ▲ Parenting issues.

Is it any wonder that the majority of Americans believe in God . . . and angels . . . and the power of prayer? We need all the help we can get (including positive friends to buoy us—check out Chapter 9!).

Add to this the fact that with middle age comes the clarion call of mortality. You may find yourself thinking about your spirituality more than ever before. In addition, as you and your friends and siblings age, it becomes increasingly difficult to find anyone without serious crises in his or her life. What do we mean? In Erica's small circle of friends and family, she has had two of her best friends face breast cancer, has a parent who is going blind, and has seen a number of marriages in serious trouble from everything from infidelity to simply serious unhappiness leading to di-

God on the 'Net

Plug in the word "God" on the Google search engine and you'll get (at least in July of 2003) 41,600,003 sites. That's a lot of God in cyberspace!

vorce. She has friends who have struggled with depression and friends whose parents have died suddenly after short illnesses. She has seen years in which she has attended way too many wakes and funerals and spent far too many hours in the Hallmark aisle struggling to find the right card to send to friends facing deep personal trials. (They don't exactly make a card for "Life sucks, but buck up!") Aging and adulthood carry with them the challenge of serious struggles as well as mankind's lifelong quest to make sense of senseless things.

Making sense of the senseless is the challenge of answering the child-like questions of faith and spirituality. What do we mean? Children have a faith that is far more upfront. When adults attend the funeral of a young person whose life was cut short tragically, they often mumble things like "such a shame" or "what a tragedy." Children say "Why did God have to let little Johnny die? WHY?" And we don't have an answer now as adults any more than we had an answer when we were 12.

So spirituality, often, has two roles in our lives. We may be looking for strength as we face suffering and pain or the difficulties of "being a grown-up" and we may long for spirituality to ease the stress of modern-day living. However, you may not feel as if you have enough time to seek spirituality, a higher power, or whatever you wish to call your God. You may be an Easter and High Holy Days kind of Christian or Jew, or you may have never stepped into the doorway of a house of faith. Yet, you may need faith and belief to give you some balance and strength in light of stress, crises, and the storms of life. It is important to seek solace from your religious faith, or, if you prefer, to get out into nature and hug a tree and make time to develop this side of your life. But can you seek spirituality? Can you make the same kind of balancing steps we have advocated in the rest of the book? Indeed, you can.

Instead of Fuzzy Thinking	Think Clearly
I want to have God more present in my life.→	I will find 10 to 15 minutes a day to be quiet and to pray or meditate.
I will go to church more often.→	I will strive to make time for my spiritual and religious belief but will understand if life events keep me from my highest ideals. I will aspire to do the best I can.

The idea of fuzzy versus clear thinking, again, is to take some measurable action. It isn't enough to "want" to be rid of something or to "want" something as vague and open ended as "faith." It also isn't helpful to have broad goals and agendas. You want to start with a manageable goal so that you can see for yourself that you are making progress. Making *time* for your spirituality is a good place to start. As busy people, for instance, you may feel as if this quest is frivolous, especially if you are a high achiever. It's not frivolous. This quest is as old as humanity, and it's an important element in the search for balance. Again, that clarion call of the soul is there for us, whether you try to drown it out with your cellphone, beeper, and Road Warrior ways or not.

OUTSIDE THE BOX

KATHY—I'll be up-front and say that I am a born-and-raised Catholic, but I seldom step into a church. I don't harbor any criticism for those that do because I believe we should all follow our own spiritual calling. My childhood memories of Catholic school consist of paddle-carrying nuns who freely walloped the heads of anyone who looked them in the eye. I remember marching a lot. When the Mother Superior told my mother that I was too curious and should go to public school, I was liberated. Even though I never connected to the teachings and rituals of the church, I always felt God around me. Over the years my sense of spirituality has grown and broadened. God is the last one I speak to each and every night.

ERICA—My spirituality gives me balance in all I do. It's a strange hybrid of Buddhism, existentialism, Christianity, and just plain old hard knocks that have taught me that in the end, there is always that "still-small voice" that will speak to you if you seek it. And no, that doesn't mean you're a schizophrenic.

Write Your Own Map

You may have been raised in a particular faith or religion. For some of us, returning to that faith is a source of comfort. Some of us may have never left it. However, for others, our childhood faith was a source of pain or guilt. In the quest for spirituality, you can give yourself permission to explore faith options that are different from those in which you were raised. Instead, you can think of this as a quest for balance, a quest for a spirituality to provide you with a foundation that will give you a sense of peace during those inevitable moments of exhaustion or crisis. It is also possible, when "writing your own map," to have goals. We don't think of having spirituality goals. A goal is seen as something to accomplish and something to achieve, like an "A" on a test or a salary raise. But it is entirely sensible to have a goal as far as your spirituality is concerned. Maybe that goal might be to purchase a book on Buddhism or some faith other than your own to gain insight into what that religion might have to offer you. Perhaps your goal might be to go back to your childhood faith by attending services with your family. You might want to "church shop" if you haven't been attending services regularly to find a church, synagogue, or mosque in your community that you might wish to attend.

What are your goals as far as a quest for spirituality? (Remember to be specific and measurable.) What issues would you like your spirituality to help you resolve?

1. ______________________________
2. ______________________________
3. ______________________________
4. ______________________________
5. ______________________________

Imagine for a moment that you have accomplished everything on your spirituality list. Answer this question:

What will your life be like when you have a newfound spirituality? How will it help you face the stresses and pressures of your life?

If spirituality has not been a part of your life, and this quest is a new one for you, think about the following question. If, however, spirituality is already a part of your life and you are seeking to make it a stronger part of your life, think of the goals you just wrote down as you reference this question.

What will be the smallest sign that you are moving in the right direction and that you are moving toward spirituality or increasing your existing faith and spirituality? You want to list this sign so that you can see your progress and recognize it.

When there is a positive change in one area, other positive changes will occur somewhere else. If you think of life as walking that tightrope, the balancing act is an art form unto itself. Without strong spirituality, you may feel as if life's problems leave you completely depleted. Spirituality can be the element of life that fills you with renewed energy when life gets you down.

The Roof Might Cave In

For some people, the quest for spirituality is as natural as breathing. Great thinkers, including Albert Einstein for instance, have believed that humankind's quest for spirituality is hardwired into our very humanness. Great thinkers believe we need spirituality.

Others, however (in particular those who have left a childhood faith), may believe "the roof will cave in" if they return to a church, synagogue, or mosque. They have a long-standing aversion to organized religion and have gotten along "fine" without it. This may well be for them. However, spirituality encompasses more than attending services in one of the world's major religions. Many people's faiths are a "hodgepodge" of beliefs and practices culled from everything from the world's major religions to some New Age theories to 12-step programs. We know people who haven't attended a church service in 20 years who still believe fiercely in guardian angels, for instance. So the quest for spirituality can take many forms.

One thing we do believe, however, is that if you are looking for balance and order in your life, spirituality can help you. If you have shut your mind to that idea, perhaps it's time to open yourself up to the possibility. This doesn't mean you are going to sell all your belongings and join a Trappist monastery. It simply means you recognize that spirituality can add something to your life. Let's list five problems or crises you are facing that a spiritual foundation might help you with.

1. ______________________________
2. ______________________________
3. ______________________________
4. ______________________________
5. ______________________________

Now it is time to be open to what spirituality can bring to your life.

Band-Aids for Bad Days

Spirituality doesn't make everything "all better." You can't go to God with a laundry list of things you'd like him to fix. That was how we often prayed as children. God was sort of like Santa Claus. You could pray for world peace, to watch over Mom and Dad . . . and while you're at it, God, could you bring me a pony.

We wish that spirituality would mean you don't have days in which all hell breaks loose. You won't ever lose your job; your mother-in-law will stop her evil ways; you won't ever have to say good-bye to someone you love; illness will never happen to anyone in your family. But that's impossible because we live in the real world with real problems. Spirituality is more like a Band-aid. It doesn't fix everything. Just like the body heals itself from a cut and the Band-aid is just there to protect the injury until you can heal. Spirituality gives you a sense of peace and balance until the elements of time and your own heart healing can make the pain of modern-day life and crises lessen.

Ready to Begin Your Quest?

Now it's time to balance your world with clear ideas of your goals in the spiritual arena.

List your top five goals toward spirituality:

1. ______________________________
2. ______________________________
3. ______________________________
4. ______________________________
5. ______________________________

Now ask yourself this question:

On a scale ranging from 1 to 10, with 1 being "the worst" and 10 being "great," how well would you say you are taking care of your spirituality right now?

____

____

If you answered with a 9 or 10, that's great. Feel good about this issue in your life. As we've said before, the fun part is that there is always more to learn. Remember that life has a way of throwing you a curve ball just when you think everything is terrific.

How have you managed to maintain your sense of balance in this area so far? What is working for you? *(Give yourself some well-deserved credit!)*

____

____

____

What could you do to bring your score up half a notch, say to a 9½? If you gave yourself a 10, what can you continue to do to keep your score at a ten?

____

____

____

____

If you feel like you wouldn't step into the door of a church and you haven't prayed since you asked God for that pony, you could still examine your spirituality:

What kinds of things have you been doing that keep your score at a two or five? Think about it—you didn't give yourself a zero so you must be doing a few things correctly. What are you doing that's right?

____

____

____

____

If you are thinking that there simply couldn't be anything positive in a score that low, you're wrong. If you didn't give yourself a flat zero it is because in some small ways you are doing a few positive things to be spiritual. It may feel small or inconsequential but change is built on tiny, but well-thought-out, steps. Just one step in the right direction is powerful because it takes you closer to your goals. You watch as your young child sleeps and have a sense—some still, small sense—that indeed there are some miracles in this life.

What is one more thing you can do to find balance in your spiritual life and bring your score up a point?

____

____

____

What will you do to ensure that you keep doing that one small thing?

____

____

How will your life be different when you manage to get your score up a few points?

____

____

What will you be doing that you are not doing now?

____

____

Who will be the most surprised about these positive changes?

____

____

____

Falling Off the Wire

Spirituality can help you walk the tightrope of life. But life will inevitably throw you some headwinds that can knock you clear off the wire. That's when spirituality can act like a net.

Time and time again, people who have come through life's darkest trials did so through some philosophy or spiritual belief that got them through it. That was their net. They may not have even realized they landed in the net until years later when they came out the other side. One of the most famous examples of this is Viktor Frankl, author of many books, but perhaps most famous for *Man's Search for Meaning* (2000). Frankl lived through the Holocaust and lost his wife and family. He also witnessed atrocities, suffered starvation, and witnessed the insanity and evilness that was the Nazi regime. Yet, through his suffering, he spawned an entire philosophical movement called logotherapy. His philosophy is not a religion in the traditional sense, but it did help him and countless others, since his book was published, make sense of the senseless. While it's hard to describe in a nutshell, and far be it from us to paraphrase a genius, at its heart it is about our humanity—and that the essence and grace of our humanity cannot be taken from us unless we give it away. He tried to walk through this world with that grace and with forgiveness.

Our spirituality can be our net in our quest for balance. It can help us on those days when we look upward and say, "God help me." He may not send a miracle to you—like always putting you in the lane that moves the fastest on your commute—but spirituality can be a breath of peace to help you in your trials.

CHAPTER 12

A BALANCED LIFE: A WORK IN PROGRESS

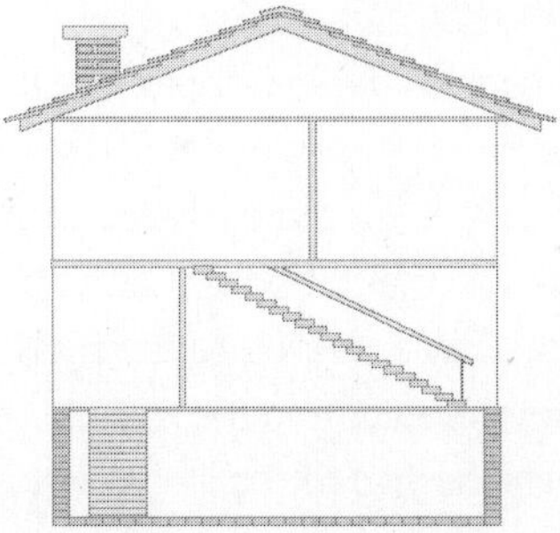

As different and unique as each one of us is, we are all the same. No matter what our calling, lifestyle, spiritual beliefs, or family background, we are all striving to live happy, fulfilling lives. We all want to have a balanced life.

We want to have all the rooms of our house in order, whether it's our inner being, relationships, career, finances, or children. When a portion of our life is out of balance, we feel thrown off course. The problem seeps into all aspects of our life, making us feel bogged down, stressed out, and despairing.

Our goal in writing this book was to create a map that will enable you to keep swaying and moving as you live your life. We all know there's no such thing as a perfect life, but there is a best one.

As much as we would like to control our world and what happens around us, we cannot. Some weeks end as uneventfully as they began, while others seem filled with unexpected headaches and catastrophes. Everyday disasters never happen at the right time. The oil burner breaks on the coldest of days. The tire goes flat when no one's around to give you a hand. Your teenager flunks math and gives you attitude when you try to talk about it. Your health insurance triples in cost and yet won't pay for anything.

How can there be a sense of balance in your life when the world seems so unpredictable? How can you stop making resolutions that go nowhere? As we close *Walking the Tightrope,* we would like to leave you with a few closing suggestions:

- *First of all, expect to do well.* Keep the expectations for your life high. Others may doubt themselves and they may even have doubts about you, but ignore them. Your life is not a script, it's yours to construct and develop as you would like.
- *Pay attention to the signs, even the small ones.* We have a tendency to hurl ourselves through our lives without noticing the signs that can guide us to the life we want to live. Your signs are all around you—in the chance encounters of the people you meet, books that catch your eye, and the song that sticks in your head. Pay attention to the signs when you are most happy, feel the most invigorated, and the most alive. Those signs are your mile-markers and can guide you to the life you most want to be living.
- *Stop doing more of the same.* So many people think that if something doesn't work that they should do more of it. If their partner doesn't listen, they should nag them more. If their children don't clean up their mess, they should be stricter. If the job is stressful, complain more. Doing more of the same is like trying to move a brick wall. If the wall won't budge, stop pushing it and try another way to get around it. If what you are doing is not working, then stop doing it and try something different.
- *Spend more energy knowing what you want, and not what you don't want.* If you know what you want, go after it. Focusing on what you don't want is negative and doesn't offer a clue as to what you can do to solve your situation. Instead of saying, "I don't want to be out of shape," say, "I want to be healthy." Focusing on the "don't wants" will never get you on your way.
- *Count your blessings.* There are blessings to be thankful for in your everyday life. Disappointments and stressors have a way of blinding us from seeing that in spite of it all, there are things to be thankful for. Be thankful for your friends, your family, the faces of your children, the person who held the door open for you at the supermarket. When you notice blessings, even the smallest ones, you begin to realize that anything really is possible.

BIBLIOGRAPHY

1. Clampitt, Cynthia (1999). *Cliff Notes: Getting Out of Debt*. Chicago: IDG Books.
2. Galinsky, Ellen, (2000). *Ask the Children: The Breakthrough Study That Reveals How to Succeed at Work and Parenting*. Quill.
3. Lederer, W. J., and Jackson, D. (1968). *Mirages of Marriage*. New York: Norton.
4. Richardson, Cheryl (2000). *Life Makeovers*. New York: Broadway Books.
5. Weiner-Davis, Michelle (1995). *Fire Your Shrink*. New York: Simon & Schuster.
6. Weiner-Davis, Michelle (2001). *The Divorce Remedy*. New York: Simon & Schuster.
7. Yager, Jan (1999). Friendships: *The Power of Friendship and How It Shapes Our Lives*. ________: Hannacroix Creek Books.
8. Yager, Jan (1999). *When Friendship Hurts: How to Deal with Friends Who Betray, Abandon, or Wound You*. New York: Fireside.

INDEX